PARENTING WITH HEART

Emotional Bonds for Early Childhood Development

SURAJIT SARKAR

INDIA : SINGAPORE : MALAYSIA

Printed By:
Notion Press Platform,
Notion Press Media Pvt Ltd,
#7, Red Cross Road,
Egmore, Chennai, Tamil Nadu 600008
www.notionpress.com

Printed in India

First Printing Edition, 2024
ISBN 979-889544489-4

To my family,

Your love, support, and wisdom have shaped the person I am today. This book is a reflection of the values and lessons passed down through generations, and it is dedicated to each of you.

Especially to my beloved nieces and nephews,

You are the inspiration behind this work. Watching you grow, laugh, and learn has been one of the greatest joys of my life. May you always be surrounded by love, and may you continue to shine brightly as the wonderful individuals you are.

With all my heart,

Surajit Sarkar

"Children may forget what you said, but they will never forget how you made them feel."

"Parenting isn't about perfection; it's about connection. Build with love, guide with empathy, and the bonds you create will last a lifetime."

Table of Contents

Preface

Parenting is one of life's most profound and rewarding journeys, yet it comes without a manual. Every parent embarks on this path with a heart full of love and a mind filled with questions. How do we raise emotionally healthy children? How do we build bonds that last? How do we guide our little ones through the complexities of their early years while ensuring they feel secure, understood, and loved?

These questions are at the heart of this book, "Parenting with Heart: Emotional Bonds for Early Childhood Development". As an educator, counselor, and parent, I have spent decades exploring the intricate dance of parenting, where emotions play a pivotal role in shaping a child's life. This book is the culmination of those years of experience, research, and heartfelt conversations with parents, educators, and children alike.

In today's fast-paced world, it's easy to become overwhelmed by the endless stream of parenting advice, much of which focuses on achieving certain milestones or fostering independence at an early age. While these goals are important, they should not overshadow the emotional foundation that is essential for a child's overall development. It is this emotional connection—the bond between parent and child—that forms the bedrock of a healthy, happy upbringing.

Throughout these pages, you'll find insights and strategies aimed at helping you nurture that bond. From understanding the importance of emotional attachment to guiding your child through their first steps of independence, this book covers the emotional milestones that are key to raising well-rounded, resilient children. You will also learn how to navigate the inevitable challenges that arise, turning moments of difficulty into opportunities for deeper connection and growth.

But this book is not just about the child; it's about you, the parent. Parenting is as much about personal growth as it is about guiding a child. It's about learning to listen, to empathize, and to love unconditionally—even on the toughest days. It's about embracing the role of a parent with heart, recognizing that the emotional bonds you build today will carry your child through life's challenges and triumphs.

"Parenting with Heart" is intended to be a companion on your journey—a source of support, encouragement, and practical wisdom. Whether you're a new parent or one with a bit more experience, I hope this book offers you insights that resonate, advice that empowers, and stories that inspire.

As you turn these pages, remember that there is no single "right" way to parent. Each family is different, and each child is unique. What remains constant is the power of love, empathy, and connection. It is my hope that this book helps you cultivate these qualities in your parenting, leading to a relationship with your child that is not only strong but also deeply fulfilling.

Thank you for allowing me to be a part of your parenting journey. May this book inspire you to parent with heart, every step of the way.

With warmth and gratitude,

Surajit Sarkar
The 17th January, 2024

Prologue

Parenting begins long before a child takes their first breath. It starts in the quiet moments of anticipation, in the dreams you have for their future, and in the silent promises you make to protect and love them. From the very beginning, parenting is an emotional journey, one that challenges, uplifts, and transforms you in ways you never imagined.

In those early days, when your baby's cries echo through the night and their tiny hand grasps your finger, you begin to understand that parenting is much more than providing for physical needs. It's about creating a bond so strong, so enduring, that it becomes the foundation upon which your child builds their world.

This bond is not formed through grand gestures, but through the everyday acts of love and care—holding them close when they're frightened, soothing their tears, and celebrating their smallest victories. It's in these moments that the emotional connection between parent and child is forged, shaping who they will become and how they will navigate the world.

But parenting is not just about the child; it's about you, too. It's about learning to trust your instincts, to grow alongside your child, and to find joy in the little things. It's about recognizing that every emotion, from the overwhelming love you feel to the frustrations that sometimes arise, is a part of this journey.

In "Parenting with Heart: Emotional Bonds for Early Childhood Development", we explore the power of these emotional connections. This book is not a guide to perfection—there is no such thing in parenting. Instead, it is a reflection on the importance of nurturing the heart of your child, of being present in their emotional world, and of building a relationship that will carry them through life's ups and downs.

As you read through these chapters, you will find practical advice, heartfelt stories, and insights drawn from years of experience. But more than anything, you will find a reminder of what truly matters: the love, empathy, and connection that define the parent-child bond.

Parenting is a journey like no other. It is filled with moments of wonder and challenge, of growth and discovery. It is my hope that this book will serve as a companion on your journey, offering support, encouragement, and a renewed understanding of the profound impact that emotional bonds have on your child's development.

So as you embark on this path, take a deep breath, hold your child close, and remember—you are not alone. Every parent walks this road, learning and growing along the way. And at the heart of it all is the unbreakable bond of love that makes every step worth it.

Welcome to the journey of parenting with heart.

Surajit Sarkar
The 17th January, 2024

INTRODUCTION

THE HEART OF PARENTING

Understanding the Emotional Core: Discover why emotions are the foundation of successful parenting.

Parenting isn't just about feeding, clothing, or sheltering a child. It's about shaping a life, molding a future. And at the core of this monumental task lies emotion. Emotions are the heartbeat of parenting. They're not mere feelings but the lifeblood that nourishes every interaction, every lesson, every moment with your child.

Imagine emotions as the soil in which your child's roots grow. Without fertile soil, a plant wilts. The same goes for children. Without the rich, nurturing environment that emotions create, a child struggles to thrive. It's in the emotional connection between parent and child that real growth happens.

Let's get down to brass tacks. Why do emotions matter so much in parenting? Because they connect. They create bonds that are stronger than any rule, more lasting than any discipline. When a child feels loved, understood, and valued, they're more likely to listen, learn, and grow. A stern word from a parent they trust carries weight. But that same word, if the emotional bond is weak, can lead to rebellion or indifference.

Think back to your childhood. Who made the biggest impact on you? Likely, it wasn't the teacher with the strictest rules or the parent with the most authority. It was the person who made you feel safe, valued, and loved. That's the power of emotion in parenting. It's the glue that holds everything together.

Let's break it down further. Emotions shape how we view the world. For a child, emotions are the lens through which they see everything. A hug after a scraped knee teaches comfort and safety. A shared laugh during a bedtime story teaches joy and connection. These aren't just moments; they're building blocks of a child's emotional foundation.

But it's not just about the happy moments. Emotions also guide us through the tough times. When a child throws a tantrum, it's not the time for logic or reason. It's a call for emotional connection. They're overwhelmed, scared, or frustrated, and they need to know they're not alone. By responding with calm, understanding, and yes, a little patience, you teach them how to navigate their own emotions. You're not just dealing with the tantrum; you're teaching them resilience, self-control, and empathy.

Here's a little story. Imagine a father, exhausted after a long day, coming home to his child who's had a meltdown over a broken toy. It would be easy to brush it off, to tell the child it's just a toy, to fix it later. But the wise father kneels down, looks his child in the eye, and says, "That must be really upsetting. I can see how much you loved that toy." Suddenly, the child's tears slowly, replaced by a nod and a sniffle. The problem hasn't changed, but the child feels understood, and that changes everything. That's the power of emotion in action.

But let's not romanticize it. Parenting isn't easy. Emotions can be messy, overwhelming, and sometimes downright frustrating. There will be moments when you're running on fumes, when the last thing you want to do is deal with another outburst, another tear. But it's in those moments that emotions matter the most. Because it's not about perfection; it's about connection. It's about showing up, even when you're tired, even when you don't have all the answers. It's about being there, really being there, in the ups and downs, the highs and lows.

Now, let's talk about the flip side. What happens when emotions are missing from the equation? Children are like mirrors; they reflect what they see. If they're met with indifference or coldness, they learn to shut down, to hide their feelings, to build walls. And those walls can be hard to break down later. A child who doesn't feel emotionally connected my struggle with self-esteem, relationships, and even learning. The stakes are high, but so are the rewards.

It's not about coddling or sheltering your child from every bump and bruise. It's about equipping them with the emotional tools they need to handle life's challenges. When a child knows they're loved, when they feel safe to express their feelings, they're more likely to take risks, to explore, to grow. They're not afraid to fail because they know they have a safety net in you.

Let's take a moment to reflect on the role of emotions in teaching. Education isn't just about facts and figures. It's about lighting a fire, sparking curiosity, and inspiring a love for learning. And how do you do that? Through emotional connection. A child who feels emotionally connected to their parent or teacher is more engaged, more curious, more eager to learn. It's not about being the smartest in the room; it's about being the most connected. That connection makes learning a shared journey, a partnership, not a chore.

Emotions also teach values. How you react in moments of stress, how you handle disappointment, how you celebrate successes—all of these teach your child about life. They're watching, learning, absorbing everything. Your emotional responses become their blueprint for handling their own emotions.

And let's not forget about the importance of play. Play is where emotions come alive. It's where children experiment, explore, and express themselves freely. It's where they learn to navigate friendships, resolve conflicts, and build empathy. Play isn't just a break from learning; it's an essential part of it. And it's fueled by emotion.

In the end, emotions are the foundation of successful parenting because they create a bond that nothing else can. They're the thread that weaves through every moment, every lesson, every day. They turn the ordinary into the extraordinary. They make parenting not just a responsibility but a joy, not just a duty but a privilege.

So, embrace the emotions. They're not a sign of weakness but of strength. They're not a distraction but the very heart of parenting.

> 99
>
> *"Tell me and I forget. Teach me and I remember. Involve me and I learn."*

And when you lead with your heart, you give your child the greatest gift of all—a deep, unshakable sense of love and belonging that will carry them through life.

A Parent's Role: Explore the impact of emotional bonds on early childhood development.

Parenting isn't just a role; it's a calling. It's the most important job you'll ever have. And at its core, parenting is about forming bonds. These bonds aren't just nice to have—they're essential. They shape your child's future in ways you can't always see, but you can certainly feel.

Let's dive into what makes these bonds so powerful. Picture a newborn cradled in their parent's arms. They don't understand words yet, but they feel. They feel warmth, love, and security. That's where it all begins. This bond is more than just physical closeness. It's emotional glue that holds your child's world together.

As your child grows, these emotional bonds act as a foundation. Every smile, every cuddle, every whispered word of comfort adds a brick to that foundation. But it's not just about making your child feel good at the moment. These bonds have a long-lasting impact, reaching far into your child's development.

Think of these bonds as the roots of a tree. The deeper and stronger the roots, the more resilient the tree. When a storm hits, a tree with strong roots might sway, but it won't fall. The same goes for your child. Life will throw challenges their way, but if their emotional roots are strong, they'll stand firm.

So, what exactly do these emotional bonds do for your child's development? For starters, they build trust. Trust isn't something that just happens; it's built over time. It's in those early moments when your child learns that you're there for them, that they can rely on you. And trust is the bedrock of any strong relationship. Without it, everything else crumbles.

But trust is just the beginning. These bonds also foster emotional intelligence. A child who feels understood and supported learns to understand and support others. They pick up on emotional cues, learn empathy, and develop the ability to manage their own emotions. In a world that often feels disconnected, these skills are priceless.

Let's talk about learning. We often think of learning in terms of ABCs and 123s, but real learning goes much deeper. It starts with curiosity, and curiosity thrives in a safe, loving environment. When a child feels secure, they're more likely to explore, ask questions, and try new things. They're not afraid to make mistakes because they know that failure isn't the end of the world—it's just a stepping stone.

Now, consider social skills. Your child's first social interactions are with you. How you respond to their needs, how you treat them, teaches them how to interact with others. If they feel loved and respected, they're more likely to show love and respect to others. They learn that relationships are built on kindness, understanding, and mutual support.

It's easy to think that children will just figure this out on their own, but that's not always the case. Children mimic what they see. If they grow up in an environment where emotions are brushed aside or ignored, they might struggle to connect with others. They might bottle up their feelings or lash out because they don't know how to express themselves.

But when you create an environment rich in emotional bonds, you give your child the tools they need to navigate life's challenges. You're not just teaching them how to survive; you're teaching them how to thrive.

There's another piece to this puzzle—confidence. A child who feels loved and supported grows up with a strong sense of self. They know who they are and what they're capable of. They're not easily swayed by others because they have a solid foundation to stand on. They're confident, but not arrogant, because their confidence is rooted in love, not in the need to prove something to the world.

Confidence, empathy, emotional intelligence—these are the gifts that emotional bonds give your child. They're not material things, but they're far more valuable. They're the qualities that will carry your child through life, no matter what obstacles they face.

And let's not forget about resilience. Life isn't always easy. There will be bumps in the road, disappointments, and heartaches. But a child who has strong emotional bonds is more likely to bounce back from these setbacks. They know that no matter how tough things get, they're not alone. They have someone in their corner, someone who believes in them.

Imagine this: Your child comes home from school after a rough day. Maybe they failed a test or had a fight with a friend. They're upset, maybe even angry. At that moment, what they need most is not a lecture or a solution. They need to feel understood. They need to know that their feelings matter. And when you provide that, you're not just comforting them; you're teaching them how to handle life's ups and downs with grace and resilience.

These bonds also play a role in physical health. Studies show that children who grow up in emotionally supportive environments are healthier. They have stronger immune systems, better stress

> **"The healthy man does not torture others—generally it is the tortured who turn into torturers. What is essential is that you nurture the child's emotional world with warmth and love, for it is this that will shape their soul."**

management, and even faster recovery from illness. It's as if emotional support is a tonic for the body as well as the mind.

So, how do you build these bonds? It's simpler than you might think. It's in the little moments—reading a book together, sharing a meal, taking a walk. It's in listening, really listening, to what your child has to say. It's in being present, even when life gets busy. It's in showing up, day after day, even when you're tired, even when you're not sure you're doing it right.

Building emotional bonds isn't about grand gestures. It's about consistency. It's about making your child feel valued every single day. It's about being their haven in a world that can sometimes be overwhelming.

But don't worry if you don't get it right all the time. No one does. What matters is that you're trying. What matters is that you care enough to keep trying. Parenting is a journey, not a destination. And on this journey, your love and emotional support are the compass that will guide your child through life.

In the end, the role of a parent isn't just to raise a child. It's shaping a human being. It's nurturing a soul. It's creating a bond that will last a lifetime, a bond that will carry your child through whatever life throws their way. That's the power of emotional bonds. That's the heart of parenting.

~~The Journey Ahead: A guide to navigating the path~~ of emotionally rich parenting.

Parenting is a journey, not a sprint. It's a long, winding road with unexpected turns and hills to climb. The goal? To raise a child who is not just good but emotionally rich, resilient, and kind. It's a path that requires heart, patience, and more than a little wisdom. So, let's talk about the journey ahead.

Picture yourself setting out on a hike. You've got your backpack, your map, and your sturdy shoes. You're excited, a little nervous, but mostly ready. This is how the journey of emotionally rich parenting begins. You start with the basics—love, patience, and understanding. These are your essentials, your compass, and your guide. But like any journey, it's the steps you take each day that make all the difference.

The first step? Be present. Parenting isn't something you can do on autopilot. It's about being there, really being there. Not just physically, but emotionally. It's about putting down the phone, turning off the TV, and focusing on the person in front of you— your child. They notice when you're paying attention. And they notice when you're not.

Think about the last time your child tried to get your attention. Maybe they pulled at your sleeve or called your name a few too many times. It's easy to brush it off, to say "just a minute," but those moments add up. Being present means showing up in those small moments, over and over again. It's not about being perfect; it's about being there, day in and day out.

Next, listen more than you speak. Kids have a lot to say, even when they're not using words. They express themselves in ways that aren't always obvious. A sigh, a frown, a tug at your hand— these are their ways of communicating. Your job is to tune in, to listen between the lines. Sometimes, what they need most is for you to hear them, without judgment, without trying to fix things. Just listen.

There's a story about a mother and her daughter. The daughter came home from school, clearly upset. The mother asked what was wrong, but the daughter didn't want to talk about it. Instead of pressing, the mother simply sat beside her, saying, "I'm here when you're ready." After a while, the daughter opened up. She didn't need advice; she needed to be heard. That's the power of listening.

As you continue on this journey, remember that emotions aren't something to be feared or avoided. They're part of being human. Your child will feel anger, sadness, frustration, and joy. It's all part of the package. Your role isn't to shield them from these emotions, but to guide them through. Teach them that it's okay to feel. It's okay to cry, to get mad, to be sad. What matters is how they handle those feelings.

When your child is upset, resist the urge to fix things right away. Instead, acknowledge their feelings. Say things like, "I can see you're really angry about this," or "It's okay to be sad." This simple act of acknowledgment validates their emotions. It tells them that their feelings are real and important.

Now, let's talk about the importance of setting boundaries. Boundaries are like the guardrails on your journey. They keep your child safe, guide their behaviour, and help them understand what's expected. But setting boundaries isn't about being strict or controlling. It's about being clear and consistent.

Imagine you're on a road trip. You need to know where you're going, right? Boundaries give your child that sense of direction. They know what's allowed and what's not. And when they test those boundaries—as all kids do—it's not a sign of disrespect. It's part of learning. It's your job to hold the line, calmly and firmly, without anger or frustration.

But here's the thing: boundaries only work when they're paired with love and warmth. A rule without a relationship leads to rebellion. Your child needs to know that even when you're firm, you're still on their side. You're still their biggest supporter, their safe place.

And then there's the matter of modeling. Children learn more from what you do than what you say. They watch you closely, picking up on how you handle stress, how you treat others, how you deal with your own emotions. If you want to raise a child who is emotionally rich, you must be willing to look at your own behaviour. How do you react when things go wrong? What do you do when you're angry or frustrated? Your child is watching, and they're learning.

So, take time for self-reflection. Ask yourself tough questions. Am I showing patience when I'm stressed? Am I treating others with kindness, even when it's hard? Am I taking care of my own emotional needs? This isn't about being perfect. It's about being honest with yourself and making the effort to grow alongside your child.

As you move forward on this journey, keep in mind that mistakes will happen. You'll lose your temper. You'll say the wrong thing. You'll miss opportunities to connect. And that's okay. What matters is how you respond to those mistakes. Apologize when you're wrong. Show your child that it's okay to mess up and that making things right is part of the process.

There's power in an apology. It shows humility, strength, and a willingness to grow. When you say, "I'm sorry," you're teaching your child that it's okay to be imperfect. You're showing them that love means owning up to mistakes and working to make things better.

Finally, let's talk about the long view. Parenting is a marathon, not a sprint. The seeds you plant today may not bloom until years down the road. But that doesn't mean the work isn't worth it. Every kind word, every act of patience, every moment of connection is a brick in the foundation of your child's future.

So, take it one day at a time. Focus on the journey, not just the destination. Enjoy the moments of laughter, the quiet times together, the shared experiences. They're the fuel that keeps you going, the rewards along the way.

Remember, you're not alone on this journey. Every parent faces challenges, doubts, and fears. But with love, patience, and a commitment to emotional richness, you can guide your child through life's ups and downs. The road may be long, but the rewards are immeasurable. Your child will grow into a person who is not just strong, but emotionally whole—a person who knows how to love, how to connect, and how to navigate the path of life with grace and resilience.

And that, my friend, is the greatest journey of all.

> **"**
>
> *"Give the ones you love wings to fly, roots to come back, and reasons to stay."*

CHAPTER ONE

EMOTIONAL ATTACHMENT

Building Bonds that Last: Learn the science and art of creating strong emotional connections with your child.

Building bonds with your child is like laying the cornerstone of a house. It's not flashy, but it's essential. These bonds are the foundation of your child's emotional life. They give them strength, resilience, and the ability to connect with others. So, let's talk about how to build these bonds—ones that will last a lifetime.

First, understand that bonding isn't a onetime event. It's not something that happens in a single moment, but rather a series of small moments strung together over time. Think of it as a mosaic. Each tile represents an interaction, a touch, a word of comfort. On its own, each tile may seem insignificant, but together, they create something beautiful and enduring.

From the very start, your child is wired to connect. Babies are born with an instinct to seek out their caregivers. They cry, they coo, they reach out with tiny hands. These are all bids for connection. How you respond to these bids matters more than anything. When you pick up your crying baby, when you smile back at their toothless grin, you're telling them, "I'm here. I see you. You matter." This is the science of attachment in action.

Let's dig into that science a bit. Psychologists have studied attachment for decades, and what they've found is simple but profound. When a child feels secure in their bond with a caregiver, they're more likely to explore the world with confidence. They know they have a safe base to return to. This sense of security comes from consistent, responsive caregiving.

It's not about getting it right every time—it's about being there, showing up, and doing your best.

But bonding isn't just about science. There's an art to it as well. The art of bonding lies in the every day. It's in the way you greet your child in the morning, the way you tuck them in at night. It's in the way you listen to them when they speak, really listen, not just wait for your turn to talk. This is where the art of connection flourishes—in those small, seemingly mundane moments that add up to something much greater.

Let's be clear: bonding doesn't mean hovering. It doesn't mean doing everything for your child or shielding them from every hurt. It means being a steady presence in their life. A lighthouse in the storm. A warm blanket on a cold night. It's about providing comfort when it's needed and stepping back when it's time for them to stand on their own.

One key to building strong bonds is through physical touch. Touch is the first language of connection. A gentle hug, a reassuring hand on the back, a playful tickle—these simple acts of touch speak volumes. They say, "You are loved, you are safe, you belong." Never underestimate the power of touch. It's a tool that can calm fears, heal hurts, and deepen your bond with your child.

But what happens as your child grows? As they become more independent, the way you connect with them will change. A toddler may cling to your leg, while a teenager might roll their eyes at a hug. This is normal. The bond is still there, but it evolves. What's important is to adapt to these changes. Find new ways to connect. Maybe it's through a shared interest, like a love for a certain sport or a passion for books. Maybe it's through quiet moments of just being together, no words needed.

Communication is another cornerstone of strong bonds. But it's not just about talking; it's about how you talk. Words can build bridges, but they can also build walls. Aim for the bridge. Speak with kindness, even when you're frustrated. Be clear, but gentle.

Remember that your child is always learning from you, especially in how you handle emotions.

Here's a story: A father and son were working on a project together, building a birdhouse. The son, eager but inexperienced, made a mistake. The father could have scolded him, but instead, he smiled and said, "That's okay. We'll figure it out together." In that moment, the father wasn't just teaching his son how to build a birdhouse—he was building something much more important. He was showing his son that mistakes are part of learning and that they don't change his father's love or support. This is the art of communication in bonding.

As your child grows, there will be times when they push you away. They might want space, or they might test boundaries. This is part of growing up. It's easy to take it personally, but try not to. Remember, the bond you've built isn't so fragile that it will break with a few arguments or slammed doors. It's like a strong, elastic band—it stretches but doesn't snap. The key is to stay calm, stay present, and keep the door open for when they're ready to reconnect.

Now, let's talk about trust. Trust is the bedrock of any strong bond. Your child needs to know they can rely on you, not just for the big things, but for the little things, too. Trust is built in the everyday moments—when you keep your promises, when you show up on time, when you listen without judgment. It's about consistency. It's about being the parent your child can count on, day in and day out.

But trust goes both ways. You also need to trust your child. Trust them to make decisions, to learn from their mistakes, to grow in their own way. This doesn't mean you let them do whatever they want. It means you give them the space to develop their own sense of self, knowing that you're there if they need you.

One final thought: bonding is a lifelong process. It doesn't end when your child leaves the nest. It continues through phone calls, visits, and shared memories. The bond you build now will carry your child through life, giving them a sense of security and belonging that they'll carry into their own relationships.

So, how do you build bonds that last? You start by showing up, by being present. You listen, you touch, you speak with kindness. You

99

"If a community values its children, it must cherish their parents."

build trust through consistency and love. And you adapt as your child grows, finding new ways to connect. It's not always easy, but it's always worth it. Because in the end, these bonds are the most valuable thing you'll ever create. They are the legacy you leave behind, the gift that keeps giving, long after the toys are outgrown and the school days are over.

Remember, building bonds with your child isn't about grand gestures. It's about the little things, done with love, over and over again. It's about the everyday moments that, when woven together, create a strong, unbreakable bond. This is the art and science of emotional attachment. And it's the most important work you'll ever do.

Why Emotions Matter in Child Development: Delve into how emotions shape your child's brain, behaviour, and future.

Emotions are the silent architects of your child's life. They shape their brain, mold their behaviour, and lay the foundation for their future. But how? Why do emotions hold such power in child development? To understand this, we need to take a closer look at what emotions do, how they work, and why they matter so much.

From the moment a child is born, emotions are at play. A newborn cries, not just to make noise, but to communicate. That cry is more than a sound; it's a signal. It says, "I'm cold," "I'm hungry," or "I need you." And when a caregiver responds, an emotional bond begins to form. This bond is crucial. It tells the baby that the world is safe, that their needs will be met. This is the first lesson in trust, and it's taught through emotion.

But emotions do more than just connect us. They also build the brain. Think of the brain as a house under construction. Emotions are the workers who lay the bricks, install the windows, and put up the walls. Without them, the house remains unfinished. Every smile, every touch, every comforting word adds a brick to the structure of the brain.

Science backs this up. Research shows that during the early years, a child's brain is incredibly malleable. It's constantly growing and changing, wiring itself based on experiences. Emotions are the electrical signals that guide this wiring. When a child feels safe and loved, their brain releases chemicals that promote growth and learning. These chemicals help form connections between neurons, which are the building blocks of thought, memory, and behaviour.

Now, let's talk about behaviour. We often think of behaviour as something separate from emotions, but they're deeply intertwined. A child's actions are often a direct response to how they feel. If they're happy, they'll smile, laugh, and play. If they're scared, they might cling to you or cry. If they're frustrated, they might throw a tantrum. Understanding this link between emotion and behaviour is key to understanding your child.

Imagine a toddler trying to build a tower of blocks. They stack one block on top of another, but the tower keeps falling over. Frustration builds. They might start to cry or throw the blocks in anger. This behaviour is a direct result of the emotion they're feeling. It's not about the blocks; it's about the frustration of not being able to make things work the way they want. As a parent, your role is to help them process that emotion. Acknowledge their frustration, offer comfort, and guide them through it. In doing so, you're teaching them how to manage their emotions, a skill that will serve them for life.

But emotions don't just influence behaviour at the moment; they also shape long-term patterns. A child who grows up in a loving, emotionally supportive environment is more likely to develop healthy behaviours. They learn to trust, to empathize, to cooperate. They learn that it's okay to feel and that it's okay to ask for help when they need it. These lessons are vital because they set the stage for future relationships, both personal and professional.

On the flip side, children who don't receive this emotional support can struggle. Without a strong emotional foundation, they may have trouble forming connections with others. They might become anxious, withdrawn, or overly aggressive. They might struggle with self-esteem, always questioning their worth because they never felt truly valued as children. These patterns can follow them into adulthood, affecting everything from friendships to careers.

So, how do emotions shape the future? The answer lies in the connections they help form. Emotions are the threads that weave the fabric of your child's life. They connect memories, experiences, and lessons learned. A happy childhood filled with love and support creates a tapestry rich in color and texture. This tapestry becomes a source of strength, resilience, and confidence that your child can draw on throughout their life.

Take empathy, for example. Empathy is the ability to understand and share the feelings of others. It's a key component of emotional intelligence, and it's something that's learned in childhood. When a parent responds to their child's needs with kindness and understanding, they're modeling empathy. The child, in turn, learns to show empathy to others. This skill is invaluable. It helps your child build strong, healthy relationships. It makes them a good friend, a caring partner, and a compassionate leader.

Another future-shaping emotion is resilience. Life is full of challenges, and how your child handles them depends largely on their emotional development. A child who has been taught to process emotions in a healthy way will be better equipped to handle setbacks. They'll understand that it's okay to feel sad or disappointed, but they'll also know that these feelings aren't permanent. They'll bounce back, ready to face the next challenge.

But perhaps the most important way emotions shape the future is through the development of self-worth. A child who feels loved and valued grows up with a strong sense of self. They know who they are, and they like who they are. This self-assurance is a gift that keeps giving. It allows them to pursue their dreams with confidence, to stand up for themselves and others, and to live a life that's true to their values.

So, how can you, as a parent, help foster these positive emotional developments? Start by being emotionally present. Be there for your child, both physically and emotionally. Listen to them, comfort them, and celebrate their successes. Show them that their feelings matter, no matter how big or small. Teach them that emotions are a natural part of life, not something to be feared or suppressed.

Also, model the behaviour you want to see. If you want your child to be kind, show kindness. If you want them to be resilient, demonstrate resilience. Children learn by watching, so make sure they're seeing the best of you.

And remember, it's never too late to start. Whether your child is a newborn or a teenager, the emotional bonds you build today will help shape their future. They will guide them through life's challenges, support them in their endeavors, and give them the strength to be their best selves.

In the end, emotions are the foundation of everything. They are the roots of the tree, the threads of the tapestry, the bricks of the house. They shape your child's brain, behaviour, and future in ways that are profound and lasting. By understanding and nurturing your child's emotions, you are giving them the greatest gift of all—a strong, healthy, and happy future. And that's why emotions matter.

> **"**
>
> *"Children are educated by what the grown-up is and not by his talk."*

The First Steps: Connecting with Your Child: Practical ways to establish trust and security from birth.

The bond between parent and child begins the moment you hold your baby in your arms. That first touch is more than skin to skin; it's heart to heart. It's where trust begins. But how do you build on that? How do you take those first steps to connect with your child in a way that builds trust and security?

It starts with being there. Not just in the room, but present in the moment. A newborn doesn't understand your words, but they feel your presence. They sense your warmth, your heartbeat, your smell. These are the things that make them feel safe. Hold them close. Let them hear your voice. Sing to them, talk to them, even if they don't understand. It's not about the words; it's about the connection.

When a baby cries, it's their way of saying, "I need you." How you respond to that cry is the first lesson in trust. When you pick them up, soothe them, feed them, or change them, you're telling them, "I'm here for you." This is how trust is built, one response at a time. It's in these small, consistent actions that your baby learns they can rely on you. This is the foundation of a secure attachment.

But connecting with your child isn't just about responding to their needs. It's also about creating moments of joy and comfort. Think of bedtime. The world outside may be dark and cold, but in your arms, your baby finds warmth and peace. Create a bedtime ritual—a quiet song, a gentle rocking, a soft blanket. These rituals become signals that it's time to rest, and that they're safe to let go of the day. Over time, these moments will not only help them sleep but also teach them that they're loved.

Touch is another powerful tool in building this connection. A gentle caress, a warm bath, a soft massage—these are ways to communicate love without words. Babies thrive in touch. It's how they explore the world, and it's how they connect with you. Make touch a part of your daily routine. It doesn't have to be elaborate. A simple stroke of the back while they drift off to sleep, a tender hand holding theirs while feeding—it all adds up. These are the first threads in the fabric of your relationship.

Eye contact is just as important. When you look into your baby's eyes, you're telling them they matter. You're saying, "I see you." And that's powerful. For a baby, who is just beginning to understand the world, knowing that they're seen is the first step to knowing they're loved. So, take a moment. Pause. Look into their eyes. Smile. This simple act can strengthen the bond between you.

But what about those times when you're tired, when the baby won't stop crying, when you feel like you've done everything but nothing seems to work? Those are the moments when connection matters most. It's easy to connect when things are going well. It's harder when you're exhausted, but that's when it's most important. Your baby needs to know that even when they're fussy, even when you're worn out, you're still there for them. This is where resilience in the relationship is built.

Consistency is key. Babies thrive on routine. They don't need surprises; they need predictability. This doesn't mean you have to have every minute planned out, but a regular rhythm to the day helps them feel secure. Feedings, naps, playtime, and bedtime— these regular events give your baby something to expect, something to rely on. And in that predictability, they find comfort.

But remember, connection is a two-way street. It's not just about you reaching out to your baby; it's about noticing when they reach out to you. When they coo, when they grasp your finger, when they nuzzle into your chest—they're trying to connect with you. Respond to these moments. Mirror their sounds, hold them close, and be present. These interactions are the building blocks of trust.

As your baby grows, so too will the ways you connect. What starts as a simple touch or a quiet song will evolve into shared laughter, play, and conversation. But the foundation you lay now—through touch, eye contact, routine, and responsiveness— will remain. These early connections are what will help your child explore the world with confidence.

Now, let's talk about your own well-being. Connecting with your child doesn't mean losing yourself in the process. It's easy to get caught up in the demands of a newborn, but it's crucial to take care of yourself too. When you're rested, when you're calm, you're better able to connect with your baby. So, don't be afraid to ask for help, to take a break when you need it. Self-care isn't a luxury; it's a necessity. Your baby needs you to be at your best.

But let's be real—there will be days when you're not at your best. There will be days when you're tired, frustrated, or just plain done. And that's okay. What matters is that you keep showing up. Your baby doesn't need you to be perfect; they need you to be there. They need to know that you're in this with them, through the good days and the hard ones.

And here's the thing: connection isn't about doing everything right. It's about being there, being real, and being human. It's about making mistakes, learning from them, and moving forward. It's about loving your baby through it all, and letting them know they're loved, no matter what.

In the end, these first steps of connection are the most important steps you'll take as a parent. They're the foundation of your child's emotional life. They're the bedrock on which trust, security, and love are built. And it's in these early moments—through touch, eye contact, routine, and presence—that you lay the groundwork for a bond that will last a lifetime.

So, take those first steps with confidence. Hold your baby close, look into their eyes, and let them know, in every way you can, that you're there for them. These are the moments that matter. These are the moments that will shape your child's world. And in the end, they're the moments you'll treasure most.

99

"A child's early emotional experiences, particularly those with their parents, lay the groundwork for all their future relationships and shape their sense of self."

CHAPTER TWO

LAYING A STRONG FOUNDATION

The Early Months: Trust and Security: Understand the importance of the first six months in shaping your child's emotional world.

The first six months of your child's life are more than just a phase. They are the bedrock upon which your child's emotional world is built. These months are critical. They set the stage for trust, security, and a sense of belonging that will last a lifetime. Understanding their importance isn't just about following a parenting manual; it's about shaping a human being.

From the moment your baby enters the world, they are looking for safety. The world is a big, strange place, and you are their anchor. Every cry, every coo, every tiny gesture is a call to connect. In these early months, your child's trust in the world begins with you. It's in the way you hold them, the way you soothe them, the way you meet their needs.

Picture this: a newborn in your arms, eyes wide open, searching for something familiar. They don't know much yet, but they know your voice, your smell, your heartbeat. These are the things that bring them comfort. When you respond to their cries, when you cradle them close, you're telling them they're safe. And in this safety, trust begins to grow.

Trust isn't built in a day. It's a process, like laying bricks to build a house. Each time you respond to your baby's needs, you add another brick. The house gets stronger, the walls taller. But what happens if you miss a brick? The house doesn't crumble, but it might have a weak spot. That's why consistency is so important in these early months. It's the regular, reliable responses that build strong trust.

Now, let's talk about the importance of touch. A baby's first language is touch. Long before they understand words, they understand the warmth of your hand, the comfort of your embrace. Skin-to-skin contact, often encouraged right after birth, is more than just a bonding experience. It's a way to regulate your baby's temperature, heart rate, and breathing. But beyond the physical, it's an emotional signal. It says, "I'm here. You're safe."

These first six months are also about learning about each other. Your baby is figuring out who you are, how you move, how you sound. And you're learning, too. You're learning what each cry means, what each squirm signifies. This mutual learning is part of building trust. It's about being in tune with each other, about creating a rhythm that works for both of you.

Feeding time is another crucial part of this bonding. Whether you're breastfeeding or bottle-feeding, these are moments of connection. It's not just about nourishment; it's about looking into your baby's eyes, holding them close, and creating a sense of calm. Your baby learns that when they're hungry, you'll feed them. When they're thirsty, you'll quench that thirst. This consistency fosters a deep sense of security.

Let's not forget about sleeping. Sleep can be a battleground for new parents, but it's also an important part of building trust. Establishing a sleep routine helps your baby know what to expect. They learn that after a bath and a lullaby, it's time to rest. This routine, repeated night after night, creates a sense of predictability that helps your baby feel secure. It's in these quiet moments, as you rock them to sleep or sit by their crib, that they learn the world is a safe place to drift off into dreams.

But what happens when things don't go smoothly? What if your baby cries for hours, and nothing seems to help? What if you're too exhausted to keep up the routine? These moments are tough, but they're also part of the process. Trust isn't about getting it right all the time. It's about being there, even when things are hard. It's about showing your baby that you'll stick with them through the rough patches.

In these first six months, your baby is also learning about emotions. They may not understand what feelings are, but they feel them intensely. When they're happy, their whole body shows it. When they're upset, they cry with their entire being. Your role is to help them navigate these big feelings. When you comfort them in their distress, you're teaching them that it's okay to feel, and that those feelings can be managed.

It's also during these early months that your baby begins to develop their first sense of independence. It might seem small, but when your baby starts to hold their head up, to reach for a toy, to roll over, they're taking their first steps toward independence. These milestones are moments of pride, but they're also opportunities to reinforce trust. When you cheer them on, when you celebrate these small victories, you're telling them that it's safe to explore, to grow, to try new things.

As your baby grows, so too will the ways you connect. The coos and cries of a newborn will give way to babbling, to smiles, to the first sounds of laughter. Each stage is an opportunity to build on the trust and security you've established. It's about being present in the moment, about recognizing the small but significant steps your baby is taking.

But remember, this isn't about perfection. It's about being human. There will be days when you're too tired, when the baby won't stop crying, when you feel like you're doing everything wrong. And that's okay. What matters is that you keep showing up. Your baby doesn't need perfection; they need you. They need to know that you're in this with them, through the good days and the bad.

In these first six months, you're not just caring for a baby; you're shaping a person. You're laying the foundation for a lifetime of trust, security, and emotional well-being. It's in the small, everyday moments—feeding, holding, soothing, playing—that this foundation is built.

So, take a deep breath. Embrace the sleepless nights, the endless feedings, the moments of doubt. Know that each of these moments is a step in building something lasting, something strong. You're not just surviving the first six months; you're creating a world where your child feels safe, loved, and ready to take on whatever comes next.

> "The bond between a parent and child is the first and most crucial relationship in a person's life. It is the foundation upon which all future relationships are built."

In the end, it's about love. Pure, simple, unwavering love. It's the thread that weaves through every feeding, every cuddle, every lullaby. It's what makes the difference in these early months. And it's what will carry your child through life, no matter what the future holds. These first six months are the beginning of a journey—a journey of trust, security, and unbreakable bonds. And it all starts with you.

Milestones in Emotional Growth: Identify key emotional milestones and how to nurture them effectively.

Emotional growth in children is like watching a flower bloom. It doesn't happen overnight, but with the right care, it unfolds naturally. Each stage is a milestone, a marker on the journey of becoming a whole person. These milestones are key to your child's development, and understanding them helps you nurture your child effectively.

The first milestone is trust. This begins in the earliest days of life, as we've touched on before. When a baby cries and you respond with care, they learn to trust the world around them. This is the foundation for all emotional growth. Without trust, nothing else can flourish. Trust tells your child that their needs matter, that they are seen, and that the world is a safe place.

As your child grows, they begin to recognize emotions. This recognition is another important milestone. You'll see it in the way they react to your smile with a smile of their own, or how they frown when they hear a loud noise. These are the first steps toward emotional understanding. Your role is to help them label these feelings. "You're happy!" or "That noise scared you, didn't it?" Naming emotions helps your child understand what they're feeling. It gives them a language for their inner world, a way to make sense of their experiences.

Around six months, another milestone emerges: the ability to express emotions. Your baby starts to show joy by laughing, displeasure by crying, and curiosity by reaching out. These expressions are raw and direct. They are your child's first attempts to communicate their feelings. Encourage this by mirroring their expressions. When they smile, smile back. When they're upset, show concern. This mirroring builds emotional resonance, helping your child feel understood and connected.

The next key milestone is separation anxiety. It typically shows up around eight to ten months. Your child begins to realize that you are a separate person who can leave and come back. This realization brings a mix of emotions. They might cry when you leave the room, cling to you more, or be wary of strangers. This is a natural part of emotional growth. It shows that your child is forming strong attachments.

To nurture your child through this stage, offer reassurance. Don't sneak away when you have to leave; instead, say goodbye with confidence. Let them know you'll be back. This helps build security. Over time, they'll learn that even when you're not there, they're still safe. It's a crucial lesson in trust and independence.

By the time your child is a toddler, they start to explore their independence. This is another big milestone. They'll begin to say "no" more often, insist on doing things themselves, and test boundaries. This is healthy. It's their way of figuring out who they are as a person. As a parent, your job is to balance their need for independence with guidance. Let them make small choices, like what to wear or which book to read. These choices empower them and help them build confidence in their own decisions.

Along with independence comes the development of empathy. Around the age of two, children start to understand that others have feelings, too. You might see this when they try to comfort a crying sibling or offer a toy to a friend. This is the beginning of empathy, a cornerstone of emotional intelligence. Encourage it by talking about feelings. "Your friend looks sad. What do you think we can do to help?" These conversations teach your child to consider others' emotions, not just their own.

As your child approaches preschool age, they begin to develop a more complex understanding of emotions. They start to see that emotions can be mixed—like feeling both excited and scared about starting school. This is a major milestone in emotional maturity. To support this growth, talk about your own feelings in a simple, clear way. "I'm happy that we're going to the park, but a little tired, too." This models emotional honesty and shows that it's okay to have more than one feeling at a time.

Another significant milestone is learning to manage emotions. This begins in early childhood and continues throughout life. You'll see your child trying to control their impulses, like when they stop themselves from hitting in frustration or wait their turn to speak. These are early signs of emotional regulation, an essential skill for navigating life's challenges.

To help your child with this, teach them coping strategies. Breathing deeply, counting to ten, or taking a break can all be useful tools. When your child is upset, guide them through these steps. "Let's take a deep breath together." Over time, they'll start to use these strategies on their own. This is how they learn to manage their emotions, rather than being overwhelmed by them.

As they grow, your child will also learn about social emotions, like pride, guilt, and shame. These emotions are tied to their sense of self and their understanding of right and wrong. They'll feel proud when they accomplish something, guilty when they've done something wrong, or ashamed if they think they've disappointed you. These feelings are part of their moral development.

Your role here is to help them navigate these emotions without being consumed by them. Praise their efforts to encourage a sense of pride, but also talk about mistakes in a way that encourages learning rather than shame. "It's okay to make mistakes; what matters is what we learn from them." This approach helps your child build a healthy sense of self-worth.

By the time your child reaches school age, they'll begin to understand more abstract emotions, like jealousy or fairness. They'll start to compare themselves to others, which can lead to new emotional challenges. At this stage, it's important to reinforce the idea that everyone has unique strengths and that it's okay to be different. Encourage them to express their feelings about these comparisons and help them find ways to cope with feelings of jealousy or insecurity.

Throughout all these stages, your presence and support are key. Emotional milestones aren't just about what your child achieves on their own; they're about the relationship you build together. It's in the daily interactions, the way you respond to their needs, and the love you show that these milestones are reached.

Remember, every child grows at their own pace. There's no rush. The milestones are guideposts, not deadlines. What matters most is that your child feels loved, supported, and understood as they navigate their emotional journey. You're there to guide them, to cheer them on, and to help them pick up the pieces when things don't go as planned.

In the end, emotional growth is about building a strong, resilient heart. It's about giving your child the tools they need to face the world with confidence, kindness, and empathy. Each milestone is a step on this journey, a piece of the puzzle that will eventually form

> **"There can be no keener revelation of a society's soul than the way in which it treats its children."**

a whole, emotionally healthy person. And as their parent, you have the privilege of being there for each and every step.

Strengthening Bonds Through Daily Interactions: Simple, everyday activities that foster a deep emotional connection.

Building a strong bond with your child doesn't require grand gestures or expensive outings. It's about the simple, everyday moments that weave the fabric of your relationship. These daily interactions are the threads that connect you and your child, creating a bond that's strong, resilient, and enduring.

Start with the morning routine. The day's first moments set the tone for everything that follows. When your child wakes up, greet them with warmth. A smile, a gentle touch, a cheerful "Good morning!"—these small acts let your child know they're loved from the moment they open their eyes. It's not just about getting ready for the day; it's about connecting before the hustle and bustle begins.

During breakfast, take the time to talk. Even if it's just a few minutes, ask your child about their dreams, what they're looking forward to today, or how they're feeling. These conversations show your child that you're interested in their thoughts and feelings. It's a way to connect over something as simple as a bowl of cereal. And in that connection, trust grows.

As you move through the day, find moments to connect, no matter how brief. If you're driving them to school, use the car ride to chat. Ask them what they're excited about or what's on their mind. If you're walking together, slow down and hold their hand. These small gestures make a big difference. They turn everyday tasks into opportunities to bond.

One powerful way to strengthen bonds is through play. Play is the language of children. It's how they explore the world, express their feelings, and connect with others. When you join your child in play, you're speaking their language. Whether it's a game of catch, building with blocks, or pretending to be superheroes, play is a way to enter your child's world. It shows them that you're not just there to guide them—you're there to share in their joy.

Mealtime is another golden opportunity for connection. It's not just about eating; it's about coming together as a family. Make it a habit to have meals together, even if it's just one meal a day. Use this time to talk, to laugh, to share stories. Ask your child about their day, listen to their stories, and share your own. These mealtime conversations help your child feel valued and understood. They create a sense of belonging, a feeling that home is a place where they're heard and loved.

Bedtime is perhaps the most intimate time of the day. It's a chance to wind down, to reflect, and to connect on a deeper level. Establish a bedtime routine that includes time for connection. It might be reading a book together, singing a lullaby, or just talking about the day. These quiet moments before sleep are when your child is most open to connection. They're relaxed, their defenses are down, and they're ready to absorb your love and reassurance.

But connection isn't just about specific activities; it's also about how you interact during everyday moments. For example, when your child asks for your attention, stop what you're doing and give it to them. Look them in the eye, listen to what they're saying, and respond with empathy. This shows them that they're important, that their thoughts and feelings matter. It's a simple act, but it reinforces the bond between you.

Another powerful way to connect is through physical touch. Hugs, high-fives, a pat on the back—these small gestures of affection build emotional closeness. They're a way to say "I love you" without words. Make it a habit to offer physical affection throughout the day. A hug before school, a cuddle on the couch, a kiss goodnight—these moments of touch create a sense of security and warmth.

Praise and encouragement are also vital in building a strong bond. When your child accomplishes something, no matter how small, celebrate it. Acknowledge their efforts and successes with genuine praise. "I'm so proud of you," "You did a great job," or "That was really kind of you" are words that build your child's self-esteem and reinforce their connection with you. Praise shows your child that you see them, that you recognize their efforts, and that you value who they are.

However, it's not just about the good times. Bonding happens in the tough moments too. When your child is upset, frustrated, or angry, how you respond matters. Instead of dismissing their feelings, acknowledge them. "I can see you're really upset," or "It's okay to feel angry" are ways to validate their emotions. By doing so, you're teaching them that it's safe to express their feelings with you. You're showing them that you'll be there for them, no matter what.

Even chores can be an opportunity to bond. Involve your child in household tasks, not just as a way to get things done, but as a way to spend time together. Whether it's setting the table, folding laundry, or watering the plants, these shared activities teach responsibility while also creating moments of connection. Working together toward a common goal, even a small one, strengthens your relationship.

Another way to deepen your bond is through shared interests. Find something you both enjoy and make it a regular part of your routine. It could be cooking together, playing a sport, or working on a hobby. These shared activities give you something to look forward to together. They create memories that will last a lifetime and give you a common ground to connect on.

Don't forget the importance of listening. When your child talks, listen with your full attention. Put away distractions, look at them, and really hear what they're saying. Listening is one of the most powerful ways to show love. It tells your child that they matter to you, that their voice is important.

Finally, remember that connection isn't about perfection. It's about being present, being real, and being consistent. It's about showing up every day, in big ways and small, to let your child know they're loved. The bond you build through these daily interactions is what will carry you through the challenges and joys of parenting. It's what will help your child grow into a confident, secure, and emotionally healthy adult.

In the end, it's the simple, everyday moments that matter most. The smiles, the hugs, the shared laughter—these are the things that strengthen the bond between you and your child. They're the foundation of a relationship that will last a lifetime. So, embrace the daily routines, the small gestures, the quiet moments. In them, you'll find the true heart of connection.

> **"**
>
> *"Give me a child until he is 7 and I will show you the man."*

CHAPTER THREE

PARENTS AS FIRST TEACHERS

Learning Through Love: How your emotional presence transforms you into your child's most important teacher.

You are your child's first teacher, but not because you stand on a blackboard or hand out worksheets. Your lessons don't come from textbooks or follow a curriculum. Instead, they flow from your love, your presence, and your everyday actions. Learning through love is about the subtle, powerful ways you shape your child's understanding of the world.

From the moment your child is born, they're soaking up everything around them. They watch your face, listen to your voice, and feel your touch. They learn that when they cry; you come. When they smile, you smile back. These simple exchanges are their first lessons in trust and communication. And they're all rooted in love.

Love is more than a feeling; it's a force that shapes your child's world. When you respond to their needs with care and attention, you're teaching them that the world is a safe place, that people can be trusted, and that they are valued. These are the first, most important lessons they'll ever learn.

But learning through love doesn't stop at infancy. As your child grows, so do the lessons. Every hug, every word of encouragement, every time you listen to them with patience and understanding, you're teaching them how to be in the world. You're showing them what it means to be kind, to be patient, to be strong.

Take, for example, a toddler learning to walk. They stumble, they fall, they get back up. Each time, they look to you for reassurance. Your smile, your outstretched hands, your gentle words of encouragement—they're all teaching your child that it's okay to fall, that trying again is part of learning, and that they're not alone in the process. This lesson goes far beyond learning to walk. It's a lesson in perseverance, in resilience, in the belief that they can overcome challenges with your support.

As your child moves into the preschool years, their learning through love continues to deepen. They start to mimic your behaviour, to imitate the way you speak, the way you react to situations. If you approach life with kindness and patience, they'll start to do the same. If you show frustration or anger, they'll pick that up too. Your emotional presence, the way you carry yourself through the ups and downs of daily life, becomes a blueprint for your child's own behaviour.

Imagine a morning where everything seems to go wrong. The toast burns, the car won't start, you're running late. At that moment, your child is watching. They're learning how to handle stress, how to manage frustration. If you take a deep breath, if you find a way to laugh off the mishaps, you're teaching them that setbacks are part of life and that they can be managed with grace. This is learning through love—showing your child how to navigate life's challenges with a steady heart.

Love also teaches empathy. When your child sees you comfort a friend who is sad, or when you listen to their worries with full attention, they're learning to care for others. Empathy isn't something that can be taught through lectures or rules. It's something that's felt, experienced, and absorbed through loving interactions. When your child feels loved and understood, they're more likely to extend that same understanding to others.

Another powerful way you teach through love is by setting boundaries. It might seem counterintuitive, but love and limits go hand in hand. When you set clear, consistent boundaries, you're teaching your child about safety, respect, and self-discipline. Boundaries aren't just rules to follow; they're lessons in how to live in a world with others. They teach your child that their actions have consequences, that they're part of a larger community, and that love sometimes means saying no.

For example, when you tell your child they can't have a cookie before dinner, you're not just enforcing a rule. You're teaching them about delayed gratification, about the importance of taking care of their body, and about trust—that you're looking out for their best interests, even when they don't understand it yet. This is love in action, shaping their understanding of the world in a way that words alone never could.

As your child grows older, the lessons of love evolve. They start to ask bigger questions, to challenge ideas, to explore their own identity. During these years, your role as their first teacher takes on new dimensions. Now, it's about guiding them through the complexities of life, helping them navigate friendships, school, and the ups and downs of adolescence.

In these moments, love becomes the anchor. It's what keeps them grounded when they're feeling lost, what gives them the courage to take risks, and what reassures them that no matter what, they have a safe place to return to. When your teenager comes home after a tough day at school, and you're there with a listening ear and a heart full of understanding, you're teaching them about resilience, about the importance of family, and about the enduring power of love.

But love doesn't just shape your child's understanding of the world; it shapes their understanding of themselves. When they feel loved, they learn that they are worthy of love. They develop a sense of self-worth that carries them through life's challenges. They learn that they don't have to be perfect to be valued, that their worth isn't tied to their achievements, but to who they are as a person.

Consider the impact of a simple phrase: "I love you." When spoken with sincerity, it's a powerful message. It tells your child that they are loved unconditionally, not for what they do, but for who they are. This message builds their confidence, strengthens their self-esteem, and gives them the courage to explore the world, knowing they are supported.

As they grow into adulthood, the lessons they've learned through your love will continue to guide them. They'll approach relationships with empathy, handle challenges with resilience, and move through the world with a sense of confidence and self-worth. The love you've shown them will become the foundation upon which they build their own lives, and eventually, the lives of their children.

In the end, learning through love is about more than just teaching your child how to read, write, or count. It's about teaching them how to be in the world, how to love themselves and others, how to face challenges with courage, and how to live a life filled with meaning and connection.

> **"There is no school equal to a decent home and no teacher equal to a virtuous parent."**

You are your child's first teacher, not because you have all the answers, but because you have love. And through that love, you're giving them the most important lessons they'll ever learn. Lessons that will stay with them long after they've left your home, shaping the person they become and the life they create.

The Power of Role Modeling: Demonstrate behaviours and values that will resonate with your child throughout their life.

Children are like sponges. They soak up everything around them—what they see, what they hear, and how they're treated. As a parent, you are the primary model for how they will behave and what they will value. Your actions, not just your words, teach them the most profound lessons. This is the power of role modeling, and it's one of the most important tools in your parenting toolkit.

Imagine you're in the kitchen, preparing dinner. Your child is playing nearby, but their eyes are on you. They see how you handle the vegetables, how you deal with a pot that's boiling over, and how you react when you drop something. If you respond with patience and calm, they learn that mistakes aren't the end of the world. If you lose your temper, they see that too. Every action, every reaction, is a lesson.

Children are keen observers. They may not always do what you say, but they will often do what you do. If you want your child to grow up with strong values and good behaviour, you must live those values yourself. This doesn't mean being perfect. It means being mindful of how your behaviour shapes theirs.

Let's start with kindness. It's easy to tell your child to be kind, but it's far more powerful to show them. When they see you treating others with respect, whether it's the cashier at the grocery store or a neighbor who needs help, they learn that kindness isn't just something you talk about—it's something you do. Hold the door for someone, say "thank you," offer help when you see a need. These small acts of kindness are the seeds that grow into a compassionate heart.

Patience is another value that children learn best through observation. Life is full of frustrations—traffic jams, long lines, technology that doesn't work as it should. How you handle these everyday annoyances teaches your child more about patience than any lecture ever could. If you take a deep breath and handle these situations with grace, your child will learn that patience is a strength, not a weakness. They'll see that staying calm in the face of frustration is possible and that it leads to better outcomes.

Integrity is one of the most important values you can model. Children are always watching, and they notice when your actions align with your words—and when they don't. If you tell your child it's important to be honest, but then they hear you lying to get out of something, they learn that honesty is optional. But if you live with integrity, if you're honest, even when it's hard, your child will learn to value truthfulness. They'll see that integrity isn't just about what you say—it's about who you are.

Responsibility is another lesson best taught by example. When your child sees you taking care of your commitments—whether it's showing up for work on time, paying bills, or keeping promises—they learn that responsibility is part of life. It's not just about doing chores; it's about being dependable, about being someone others can count on. When you take responsibility for your actions, especially when you make a mistake, you show your child that accountability is a sign of strength, not weakness.

Modeling a positive attitude is also crucial. Life isn't always easy, and there will be times when things don't go your way. How you react in those moments teaches your child how to deal with adversity. If you approach challenges with a positive outlook, with a mindset of "we can get through this," your child will learn to do the same. They'll see that a positive attitude doesn't mean ignoring problems; it means facing them with hope and resilience.

Consider how you handle relationships. Your child watches how you interact with your partner, your friends, and your family. They notice if you listen when others speak or if you interrupt. They see if you argue with respect or with anger. These observations shape their understanding of how relationships work. If you want your child to build healthy, respectful relationships, you need to model those behaviours in your own life. Show them that love is about more than just words—it's about actions, about listening, about being there for the people you care about.

Self-care is another important lesson to model. It's easy to get caught up in taking care of everyone else, but your child needs to see that taking care of yourself is important too. When you make time for exercise, for rest, for the things that bring you joy, you teach your child that self-care isn't selfish—it's necessary. They learn that it's okay to say no sometimes, that it's important to set boundaries, and that taking care of their own needs will help them take better care of others.

Forgiveness is a value that's best taught through example. Everyone makes mistakes, including you. How you handle those mistakes, how you forgive yourself and others, teaches your child how to deal with their own missteps. If you hold grudges, they'll learn to do the same. But if you forgive, if you let go of anger and move forward, they'll see that forgiveness is a part of love, a way to heal and to grow.

Perhaps one of the most challenging lessons to model is dealing with emotions. Your child learns how to handle their own feelings by watching how you handle yours. If you bottle up your emotions, they might learn to do the same. But if you express your feelings in a healthy way—talking about them, finding constructive outlets for frustration or sadness—they'll learn that emotions are a natural part of life and that it's okay to express them.

Think about the language you use. Children pick up on your words, but also on your tone, your body language, the way you speak about yourself and others. If you speak with kindness and respect, if you avoid gossip and negative talk, your child will learn to do the same. They'll learn that words have power, that they can build up or tear down, and that it's important to choose them wisely.

But role modeling isn't just about what you do in front of your child. It's also about how you treat yourself. If you're kind to yourself, if you give yourself grace when you make a mistake, your child will learn to be kind to themselves too. They'll learn that self-compassion is as important as compassion for others, and that treating themselves with love and respect is part of living a happy, healthy life.

> *"It is easier to build strong children than
> to repair broken men."*

In the end, the power of role modeling is in the consistency of your actions. It's about being the person you want your child to become. It's about showing them, every day, what it means to live with integrity, kindness, and love. Your child might not always listen to what you say, but they're always watching what you do. And what they see in you will shape who they become.

So, live the values you want to pass on. Be the person you want your child to grow up to be. Because in the end, your actions will echo through their life, long after they've left your home. And that's the true power of role modeling.

Turning Daily Activities into Lessons: Use routine tasks as opportunities to teach life skills and emotional intelligence.

Life is full of routine tasks. The daily grind of chores, errands, and responsibilities. But within these ordinary moments lies the opportunity to teach your child valuable lessons. Every task, no matter how small, can become a lesson in life skills and emotional intelligence. It's not about adding more to your plate; it's about using what's already there.

Take, for instance, the simple act of cooking a meal. On the surface, it's just about preparing food. But look closer, and you'll see the chance to teach patience, responsibility, and teamwork. Invite your child into the kitchen. Let them stir the sauce, chop vegetables (with supervision, of course), or set the table. As they help, talk about what you're doing and why. Explain that cooking takes time, that the following steps in order matters.

When they see the meal come together, they'll learn that patience and effort lead to something rewarding.

Mealtime itself is another routine that's rich with teaching moments. Use this time to teach gratitude and mindfulness. Before eating, take a moment to express thanks for the food on the table. This small gesture instills a sense of appreciation. During the meal, encourage your child to talk about their day. Ask them what they enjoyed, what challenged them, and what they learned. These conversations build emotional intelligence by helping your child reflect on their experiences and express their feelings.

Chores are another goldmine for lessons. It's easy to see them as just tasks that need to get done, but they're much more than that. When your child helps with chores, they learn responsibility and the value of contributing to the family. Whether it's folding laundry, sweeping the floor, or feeding a pet, each chore is an opportunity to teach them how to care for their environment and for others.

Make chores a shared activity. Work alongside your child, turning what could be a dull task into a time of connection. Talk as you work, and use the time to teach skills like organization and time management. For example, if you're cleaning up toys, show your child how to sort them by type or size. Explain that putting things away in the right place makes it easier to find them later. This simple lesson teaches order and foresight.

Errands, too, can become lessons. A trip to the grocery store is a chance to teach your child about planning, budgeting, and making healthy choices. Before you go, involve them in making a shopping list. At the store, let them help find items on the shelves. Talk about why you choose certain foods over others—because they're nutritious, because they're on sale, or because they're needed for a recipe. This teaches your child to think critically about their choices and to understand the reasons behind them.

Handling money is another important skill that can be woven into daily activities. Whether it's paying for groceries, giving an allowance, or saving for something special, use these moments to teach financial literacy. Explain the concept of money, how it's earned, and why it's important to save. If you're paying with cash, let your child count out the bills or change. If you're using a card, explain how it works. These small lessons build a foundation of financial understanding that will serve them well in the future.

Routine tasks can also teach empathy and kindness. For example, when you're running errands, point out acts of kindness you see—someone holding a door open, a cashier smiling at a customer, or someone helping another with their bags. Talk about why these actions matter. Encourage your child to look for opportunities to be kind themselves. It might be something as simple as saying "please" and "thank you," or it could be offering to help someone in need. These small acts teach your child that kindness is a part of everyday life.

Even the ride to school can be a time for learning. Use the drive to talk about the day ahead. Ask your child what they're excited about, what they're nervous about. These conversations help them prepare mentally and emotionally for what's coming. If they're anxious about something, talk through it. Help them find solutions or ways to cope. This teaches problem-solving and emotional resilience.

Bedtime is another routine rich with potential. It's a time for winding down, but also for reflection and connection. Use bedtime stories to teach values and life lessons. Choose books that illustrate the importance of honesty, courage, or friendship. After reading, talk about the story. Ask your child what they thought, what they learned, and how they might apply those lessons in their own life. This not only fosters a love of reading but also teaches critical thinking and moral reasoning.

The bedtime routine itself is a lesson in self-care. Brushing teeth, washing up, and getting enough sleep are all habits that contribute to a healthy lifestyle. By making these activities a regular part of the evening, you teach your child the importance of taking care of their body. Over time, these routines become ingrained, setting the stage for lifelong healthy habits.

Even the simplest moments can be teaching moments. Take, for example, a rainy day. Instead of seeing it as a setback, turn it into an opportunity for creativity. Build a fort out of blankets, play a board game, or try a new craft. These activities teach your child to find joy in the little things, to be resourceful, and to adapt when things don't go as planned.

Another everyday moment ripe for learning is during transitions—getting ready for school, moving from playtime to dinnertime, or settling down for bed. Transitions can be tricky for children, but they're also opportunities to teach time management and adaptability. Help your child learn to anticipate what's next by giving them a heads-up—"In five minutes, we'll start getting ready for bed." This helps them prepare mentally for the change, making transitions smoother and teaching them to manage their time and expectations.

Life is full of routines, and within those routines are countless opportunities to teach your child. You don't need to create elaborate lessons or carve out special time to teach life skills and emotional intelligence. The lessons are already there, woven into the fabric of your day. It's about recognizing those moments and using them to guide your child's growth.

In the end, it's these everyday lessons that will stick with your child. The skills they learn while folding laundry, the values they absorb during bedtime stories, the empathy they develop while running errands—these are the lessons that shape who they become. They're not just learning how to complete tasks; they're learning how to navigate life with confidence, kindness, and resilience.

"Children have never been very good at listening to their elders, but they have never failed to imitate them."

So, embrace the routines. See the daily grind not as a chore, but as a classroom. Your child is always learning, and every moment is a chance to teach them something valuable. Through these simple, everyday activities, you're not just getting through the day—you're building the foundation for your child's future. And that's a lesson worth teaching.

CHAPTER FOUR

EMOTIONAL EDUCATION

Teaching Rational Relationships: Balance love and discipline to cultivate a healthy, respectful relationship with your child.

Parenting is a balancing act. You walk a tightrope between love and discipline every day. Too much of one, and you risk spoiling your child. Too much of the other, and you might distance them. Finding that balance is key to building a healthy, respectful relationship with your child. It's about teaching them how to navigate the world with both heart and mind.

Love is the foundation. It's the bedrock of your relationship with your child. Without love, discipline becomes harsh, even cruel. But love alone isn't enough. It needs structure, boundaries, and guidance to help your child grow into a responsible, thoughtful person. Discipline, when done right, isn't about punishment—it's about teaching. It's about helping your child understand consequences, develop self-control, and learn respect.

Let's start with the basics. Love your child openly and fully. Show them affection daily, not just when they've done something right, but because they exist. Hugs, kind words, and simple acts of care go a long way. These gestures create a sense of security and belonging. When your child feels loved, they're more likely to listen, to cooperate, and to respect the rules you set. They're not afraid of discipline because they know it comes from a place of love.

But love isn't about letting your child do whatever they want. It's about setting boundaries that keep them safe and help them learn. Boundaries teach your child that their actions have consequences. They learn that the world isn't just about them, that other people's needs and feelings matter too.

Imagine your child is playing with toys and refuses to share with a sibling. Here's where the balance between love and discipline comes in. You could let it slide because you don't want to upset them. But that doesn't teach them anything. Or you could get angry, scold them harshly, and take the toys away. But that might only create resentment. Instead, you calmly explain why sharing is important, why their sibling's feelings matter, and what will happen if they don't share. This approach teaches them empathy, fairness, and respect, all while reinforcing that love and discipline can coexist.

Discipline should always be consistent. Inconsistency confuses your child and makes them feel insecure. If the rules change depending on your mood, your child won't know what to expect, and they might test boundaries more often to see what they can get away with. Consistent discipline, on the other hand, builds trust. Your child knows where the lines are, and they learn to respect them. It shows that you mean what you say, that you're reliable, and that you're in control—not in a domineering way, but in a protective, guiding way.

However, consistency doesn't mean rigidity. Life isn't black and white, and parenting shouldn't be either. There are times when flexibility is needed. Maybe your child is having a rough day, or there's something going on that makes sticking to the rules too hard for them at that moment. Being able to bend without breaking shows your child that you understand them, that you're fair, and that rules exist to guide them, not to control them.

When enforcing discipline, it's important to focus on the behaviour, not the child. Saying "You're a bad boy" when your child misbehaves attacks their character, which can damage their self-esteem. Instead, say something like, "That was not a good choice" or "What you did was hurtful." This approach separates the action from the person, allowing your child to understand that it's their behaviour that needs to change, not who they are.

And when discipline is necessary, it should be proportional. The punishment should fit the crime. Taking away all privileges for a small infraction is excessive and teaches your child to fear you, rather than to learn from their mistakes. A time-out, a loss of a toy for a day, or an extra chore are often enough to make the point without going overboard. The goal of discipline is to correct behaviour, not to make your child feel powerless or unloved.

After discipline, reconnect with your child. Once the time-out is over or the privilege is restored, show them that all is forgiven. Give them a hug, a smile, or a kind word. Let them know that while you didn't approve of their behaviour, your love for them hasn't changed. This teaches them that while actions have consequences, love is constant.

Part of balancing love and discipline is teaching your child about self-discipline. This means helping them develop the ability to control their impulses, delay gratification, and think before they act. You do this by modeling the behaviour yourself. When your child sees you staying calm in a stressful situation, finishing your work before relaxing, or treating others with respect even when you're upset, they learn to do the same.

Self-discipline also comes from giving your child responsibilities. Chores, homework, and other tasks teach them that they have obligations, that life requires effort, and that rewards come from work. When they complete these tasks, praise their effort, not just the outcome. This reinforces the idea that doing the right thing, even when it's hard, is what matters.

Another key aspect of teaching rational relationships is communication. Talk to your child about why rules exist, why certain behaviours are expected, and what the consequences of their actions are. Explain things in a way they can understand, based on their age and maturity. When they understand the "why" behind the rules, they're more likely to follow them and to respect you for setting them.

But communication isn't just about explaining rules; it's also about listening. Make sure your child knows they can come to you with their problems, fears, or mistakes without being immediately judged or punished. If they feel they can talk to you, they're more likely to open up and seek guidance before making a bad decision. This openness is crucial for building a relationship based on respect and trust.

Finally, remember that teaching rational relationships is a long game. Your child won't learn everything in a day, a week, or even a year. It's a process that takes time, patience, and consistency. There will be setbacks, days when you feel like nothing is getting through. But each moment you spend balancing love and discipline is a step toward helping your child grow into a responsible, respectful, and emotionally intelligent person.

> **"The emotional brain responds to an event more quickly than the thinking brain."**

In the end, the goal of balancing love and discipline isn't to create a perfectly obedient child. It's fostering a relationship where your child feels secure, respected, and loved, even when they make mistakes. It's about teaching them that while there are rules in life, those rules are there to guide them, not to control them. And that at the center of it all, love remains constant, a steady force that guides both you and your child through the challenges and joys of life.

Cultivating Emotional Intelligence: Equip your child with the tools to understand and manage their emotions effectively.

Emotional intelligence is the compass that guides us through life. It helps us understand our feelings, manage them, and connect with others. For your child, developing emotional intelligence is as essential as learning to read or count. It's the skill set that will help them navigate friendships, handle conflicts, and face life's ups and downs with resilience.

But how do you cultivate emotional intelligence in your child? It starts with understanding that emotions are neither good nor bad. They simply are. Emotions are signals, messages from within that tell us how we're reacting to the world around us. Teaching your child to recognize and understand these signals is the first step in building emotional intelligence.

Begin with the basics: naming emotions. Young children often don't have the words to describe what they're feeling. They might cry out of frustration, throw a tantrum out of fear, or become quiet when they're sad, but they don't always know why. Your job is to help them put words to those feelings. When your child is upset, say, "I see you're feeling angry" or "It seems like you're sad." This simple act of naming emotions gives your child a way to express themselves. It turns a swirl of feelings into something they can understand and talk about.

Once your child can name their emotions, the next step is teaching them to understand where those feelings come from. Ask questions like, "What happened that made you feel this way?" or "Why do you think you're feeling like this?" These questions encourage your child to reflect on their experiences and understand the connection between events and emotions. This process of reflection helps them see that emotions are responses to what's happening around them, not just random feelings that appear out of nowhere.

But recognizing emotions is only half the battle. The real challenge lies in managing them. Emotions can be overwhelming, especially for a child. They need tools to help them cope when feelings get too big to handle. One of the most effective tools is deep breathing. It's simple, but powerful. When your child is upset, guide them through a few deep breaths. "Breathe in slowly through your nose, hold it for a moment, then breathe out through your mouth." This calms the body and gives them a moment to pause before reacting. It's a technique they can use throughout their life to stay grounded when emotions run high.

Another tool is teaching your child to take a break when they're feeling overwhelmed. Sometimes, the best way to manage an emotion is to step away from the situation that's causing it. Encourage your child to take a moment alone when they need it. Maybe they can go to their room, play with a favorite toy, or listen to some calming music. The goal is to give them space to cool down and think before they act. This teaches them that it's okay to feel emotions, but that they don't have to be ruled by them.

Problem-solving is another critical skill in managing emotions. When your child is faced with a challenge, help them think through solutions. Ask them, "What can we do to make this better?" or "How do you think we can solve this problem?" By guiding them to find their own solutions, you're teaching them that they have control over their emotions and their actions. They learn that while they can't always control what happens to them, they can control how they respond.

Empathy is also a cornerstone of emotional intelligence. It's the ability to understand and share the feelings of others. Children naturally start to develop empathy as they grow, but it's a skill that can be nurtured. Encourage your child to think about how others might feel in different situations. When reading a story together, ask, "How do you think that character feels?" or "What would you do if you were in their place?" These questions help your child put themselves in someone else's shoes, fostering empathy and compassion.

Modeling is another powerful way to teach emotional intelligence. Your child learns by watching how you handle your own emotions. If you stay calm under pressure, they'll learn to do the same. If you express your feelings in a healthy way, they'll follow your lead. Talk about your emotions with your child. If you're frustrated, say, "I'm feeling frustrated right now because…" and explain how you're dealing with it. This shows your child that it's okay to have emotions, and that there are healthy ways to manage them.

Teach your child about the importance of expressing emotions, not just the good ones, but the difficult ones, too. It's important for them to know that it's okay to be sad, angry, or scared. What matters is how they express those feelings. Encourage them to talk about their emotions rather than acting them out. If they're upset, ask them to use their words instead of yelling or hitting. This teaches them that communication is key to resolving conflicts and that their feelings are valid, even when they're tough.

Another aspect of emotional intelligence is learning to accept and learn from emotions. Sometimes, feelings can be uncomfortable, but that doesn't mean they're bad. Help your child understand that emotions are temporary and that they can learn something from every experience. If they're disappointed, for example, talk about what they can learn from that situation. Maybe it's a lesson in patience, or maybe it's about finding new ways to reach a goal. By reframing emotions as opportunities for growth, you're teaching your child resilience.

Finally, it's important to celebrate emotional intelligence. Recognize and praise your child when they handle a situation well. If they solve a problem on their own, show empathy, or manage their emotions in a healthy way, let them know you noticed. "I'm really proud of how you handled that," or "You did a great job staying calm," reinforces their efforts and encourages them to keep practicing these skills.

In the end, cultivating emotional intelligence is about giving your child the tools they need to understand themselves and others. It's about teaching them that emotions are a natural part of life, not something to be feared or ignored. With these tools, your child will be better equipped to handle whatever life throws their way. They'll be able to build strong relationships, face challenges with confidence, and navigate the complexities of life with grace and empathy. And that's a gift that will serve them for a lifetime.

> *"When educating the minds of our youth, we must not forget to educate their hearts."*

Communication that Connects: Techniques for fostering open, honest, and emotionally supportive dialogue with your child.

Communication is the lifeline of any relationship, and when it comes to your child, it's the thread that weaves your bond together. But good communication doesn't happen by accident. It's something you build, moment by moment, with intention and care. It's about creating a space where your child feels heard, valued, and understood. Let's talk about how you can foster open, honest, and emotionally supportive dialogue with your child.

First, it's important to listen. Really listen. This might sound simple, but in practice, it's one of the hardest things to do. Listening isn't just about hearing the words your child is saying. It's about tuning into their emotions, reading between the lines, and paying attention to their body language. When your child talks to you, put down your phone, turn off the TV, and give them your full attention. Look them in the eyes. Nod your head. Let them know you're fully present. This shows them that what they're saying matters to you, and it encourages them to keep talking.

But listening also means being patient. Children don't always have the words to express what they're feeling. Sometimes, they stumble through their thoughts or take a long time to get to the point. Resist the urge to finish their sentences or rush them along. Give them the time they need to find the right words. Your patience teaches them that it's okay to take their time, that their voice is worth hearing.

Next, ask open-ended questions. Instead of questions that can be answered with a simple "yes" or "no," ask questions that invite more conversation. Instead of "Did you have a good day?" try, "What was the best part of your day?" or "What did you do today that made you happy?" These types of questions encourage your child to share more about their experiences and feelings. They open the door to deeper conversations and help you get to know your child better.

It's also important to create a judgment-free zone. If your child feels like they'll be judged or criticized for what they say, they'll shut down. They'll keep their thoughts and feelings to themselves, and the lines of communication will close. To prevent this, make sure your child knows that they can talk to you about anything—without fear of being judged. If they come to you with a problem or a mistake, focus on listening and understanding first. Save the advice or discipline for later. Your goal is to create a safe space where your child feels comfortable sharing their true thoughts and feelings.

When your child does share something difficult with you, resist the urge to immediately offer solutions. Sometimes, they just need someone to listen, to acknowledge their feelings, and to validate their experience. If they're upset about something, say things like, "That sounds really tough," or "I can see why you're feeling that way." This shows them that you're not just hearing their words, but you're also understanding their emotions.

Another key to fostering open communication is to share your own thoughts and feelings with your child. This doesn't mean burdening them with adult problems, but rather, showing them that it's okay to talk about emotions. If you're having a tough day, you might say, "I'm feeling a little stressed today, but I'm working through it." This models healthy communication and shows your child that it's normal to talk about how we feel.

Humor can also be a powerful tool in communication. Laughter breaks down walls and makes difficult conversations easier. If your child is struggling to open up, try lightening the mood with a bit of humor. A shared joke or a funny story can create a sense of connection and ease any tension. It's a reminder that conversations don't always have to be serious to be meaningful. Humor shows your child that communication can be enjoyable, not just something reserved for problems or lectures.

Another important aspect of communication is honesty. Children are perceptive. They can tell when you're not being truthful, and that can erode trust. Being honest with your child, even when it's uncomfortable, sets a strong foundation for your relationship. If they ask a tough question, answer it as truthfully as you can, in a way that's appropriate for their age. If you don't know the answer, admit it. Saying, "I'm not sure, but we can figure it out together," shows that you respect them enough to be honest and that you're willing to learn alongside them.

Timing is also crucial in communication. Sometimes, the best conversations happen when you least expect them—during a car ride, while cooking dinner, or at bedtime. These are the moments when your child might feel more relaxed and open to talking. Be available for these spontaneous chats. You don't always need to schedule a "talk." Sometimes, just being present and open to conversation is enough to invite meaningful dialogue.

Respect your child's privacy and boundaries, too. There will be times when they might not be ready to talk, and that's okay. Let them know that you're there when they're ready, but don't push them to open up before they're comfortable. Respecting their space shows them that you trust them to come to you when they're ready and that you value their autonomy.

It's also important to avoid overreacting. If your child comes to you with something shocking or upsetting, try to stay calm. If you react with anger or panic, they might be less likely to come to you in the future. Take a deep breath, listen to what they're saying, and respond with empathy. This helps keep the lines of communication open and reinforces that you're a safe person to talk to, no matter what the issue is.

Encourage your child to express themselves creatively, too. Sometimes, children struggle to find the right words to express their emotions. Art, music, or writing can be powerful outlets for feelings that are hard to verbalize. If your child enjoys drawing, encourage them to draw how they're feeling. If they like writing, suggest they keep a journal. These activities can be a way for them to communicate their emotions in a different, often more comfortable, medium.

Finally, remember that communication is a two-way street. It's not just about getting your child to talk—it's about building a relationship where both of you feel heard and understood. Be open to feedback from your child. If they tell you that something you're doing makes it hard for them to talk to you, listen to that feedback and adjust accordingly. This shows them that their opinions matter and that you're committed to improving your relationship.

In the end, communication that connects is about more than just talking. It's about creating a bond built on trust, respect, and understanding. It's about being there for your child, not just as a parent, but as a confidant, a listener, and a friend. By fostering open, honest, and emotionally supportive dialogue, you're giving your child the tools they need to navigate their emotions, build strong relationships, and feel secure in who they are. And that's a gift that will last a lifetime.

"*The greatest sign of success for a teacher... is to be able to say, 'The children are now working as if I did not exist.'*"

CHAPTER FIVE

FAMILY MATTERS

The Power of Collaborative Parenting: How involving the whole family enhances your child's emotional development.

Raising a child is like building a house. You need strong walls, a solid roof, and a firm foundation. But you don't build it alone. You need hands to help, each person playing a part. This is where collaborative parenting comes in. When the whole family is involved, the structure becomes stronger, and your child's emotional world thrives.

Collaborative parenting means that everyone has a role to play. It's not just mom and dad setting the rules or offering comfort. It's grandparents, siblings, aunts, uncles, and sometimes even close friends. Each person brings something different to the table, adding layers of support and love that help your child grow.

Let's start with the role of extended family. Grandparents often bring wisdom and experience. They've raised children before, and they know the ropes. But more than that, they bring a sense of history and tradition. They tell stories of the past, share recipes, and pass down values. These connections give your child a sense of belonging, a feeling that they're part of something bigger. When grandparents are involved, children learn that they're rooted in a family that spans generations, which helps them feel secure and loved.

Siblings also play a crucial role in collaborative parenting. The bond between siblings is like no other. It's a relationship filled with shared experiences, laughter, and, yes, sometimes arguments. But through these interactions, children learn important life skills. They learn how to share, how to compromise, and how to support each other. When parents encourage positive sibling relationships, they help their children develop empathy, patience, and a sense of responsibility. A sibling can be a playmate, a confidant, and a lifelong friend. And in the process, they teach each other about loyalty, kindness, and cooperation.

But collaborative parenting isn't just about what the extended family and siblings bring. It's about how the family as a whole works together. When everyone is on the same page, it creates a consistent environment. Children thrive on consistency. When the rules are the same at mom's house, at dad's house, and at grandma's house, it eliminates confusion. The child knows what to expect, which fosters a sense of security.

This consistency doesn't mean that every household has to be exactly the same. Different family members may have different approaches to certain situations, and that's okay. What's important is that the core values remain consistent. Respect, kindness, and honesty should be at the heart of every interaction. When these values are shared across the family, children learn that these principles are universal, not just something that mom and dad talk about.

Communication is key to making collaborative parenting work. Families need to talk to each other, share ideas, and agree on how to handle various situations. This doesn't mean there won't be disagreements. There will be. But when families communicate openly and respectfully, they can find solutions that work for everyone. This teaches children that problems can be solved through dialogue, that everyone's opinion matters, and that working together leads to better outcomes.

Collaborative parenting also means involving your child in the family dynamics. Give them a voice. Let them express their opinions and feelings. This doesn't mean they get to make all the decisions, but it does mean they should feel heard. When children are involved in family discussions, they learn that they're valued members of the family. They learn how to articulate their thoughts, listen to others, and contribute to group decisions. This sense of inclusion boosts their self-esteem and teaches them the importance of cooperation.

Another benefit of collaborative parenting is that it provides multiple role models for your child. Each family member brings different strengths and qualities. A grandfather might show the value of hard work, while an aunt might model creativity and kindness. A sibling might teach perseverance or the joy of play. When children see these different traits in action, they learn that there's more than one way to be successful in life. They see that they can be strong, kind, creative, and hardworking, all at the same time.

But what happens when family members don't agree on parenting approaches? It's bound to happen, and that's where compromise comes in. Families need to find a middle ground that respects everyone's perspective while keeping the child's best interests at heart. Sometimes, this means letting go of small disagreements and focusing on the bigger picture. It means recognizing that there's no single "right" way to parent, and that flexibility is part of the process.

Collaborative parenting also offers support for parents. Raising a child is challenging, and doing it alone can be overwhelming. When the whole family is involved, parents have a network of support. They can lean on grandparents for advice, siblings for help with childcare, and other relatives for emotional support. This shared responsibility eases the burden of parents and allows them to be more present and patient with their child. When parents feel supported, they're better able to provide the love and guidance their child needs.

Moreover, children learn by example. When they see their family working together, they learn the importance of teamwork. They see that people can come together to solve problems, that support goes both ways, and that being part of a family means helping each other out. These lessons are invaluable. They prepare your child to build strong relationships, both within the family and in the outside world.

But collaborative parenting isn't just about handling challenges together. It's also about celebrating together. Family milestones, achievements, and even small victories are more meaningful when shared. When a child sees the whole family celebrating their achievements, they feel a deeper sense of pride and accomplishment. These shared moments create lasting memories and strengthen the bonds between family members.

In the end, collaborative parenting is about creating a network of love and support around your child. It's about showing them that they're not alone, that they're part of something bigger, and that their family will always be there for them. This sense of belonging and security is the foundation of emotional development. It helps your child grow into a confident, compassionate, and resilient person.

> *"There is no doubt that it is around the family and the home that all the greatest virtues... are created, strengthened, and maintained."*

So, involve the whole family. Encourage open communication, share responsibilities, and celebrate together. By doing so, you're not just raising a child—you're building a strong, connected family that will support each other through life's challenges and joys. And in that supportive environment, your child's emotional development will flourish.

~~Grandparents: Wisdom and Warmth: The unique role~~ grandparents play in imparting values and emotional security.

Grandparents hold a special place in the family. They are the bridge between the past and the present, carrying with them a wealth of experience and wisdom that only time can bring. Their role in a child's life is unique, offering a blend of love, guidance, and emotional security that no one else can provide.

Imagine the warmth of a grandparent's embrace. It's not just a hug; it's a connection to generations past, a reassurance that there is a steady hand to guide you, even when the world feels uncertain. This warmth is something only grandparents can give. They've been through life's ups and downs, and they've come out the other side with a calmness that helps to soothe the anxieties of youth.

Grandparents are often seen as the keepers of family traditions. They pass down stories of the family's history, share recipes that have been in the family for generations, and teach the values that have stood the test of time. These aren't just stories or meals; they're lessons wrapped in the familiarity of family, teaching children where they come from, and giving them a sense of identity.

Consider the simple act of baking cookies together. To a child, it might just be a fun activity, but to a grandparent, it's an opportunity to teach patience, share memories of their own childhood, and pass on the importance of spending time with loved ones. Each ingredient measured, each story told, adds another layer to the bond between grandparent and grandchild.

The wisdom grandparents impart isn't just in the stories they tell, but in the way they live their lives. They've learned to prioritize what truly matters—love, kindness, and understanding. They know that the small things, like a kind word or a shared moment, often mean the most. When children see their grandparents living with this wisdom, it leaves a lasting impression. It teaches them to value relationships over material things, to find joy in simple pleasures, and to approach life with a generous heart.

But it's not just wisdom that grandparents offer; it's also a deep well of emotional security. In the fast-paced world of modern parenting, where schedules are packed and stress runs high, grandparents often provide a much-needed sense of calm. They're not as worried about the latest trends or milestones; they're focused on the bigger picture. This calm presence helps children feel safe and loved, no matter what else is going on in their lives.

Think about the comfort a child feels when they visit their grandparents' house. It's often a place of stability and routine, where things move a little slower and there's always time for a game of cards or a walk in the garden. These moments of calm are more than just a break from the hustle and bustle; they're a reminder that love doesn't have to be rushed, that some of the best things in life happen when we slow down and just be together.

Grandparents also offer a different perspective on life. They've lived through different times, seen the world change, and adapted to those changes. This perspective can be invaluable to children as they learn about the world. Grandparents can share stories of how things were done in the past, providing a broader context for understanding the present. They can also offer advice that comes from experience, not just theory. When a grandparent talks about overcoming challenges or finding happiness in difficult times, it's not just talk—it's a lived experience.

This perspective is particularly important when it comes to teaching values. While parents are often focused on the day-to-day tasks of raising a child, grandparents can step back and see the bigger picture. They can reinforce the values that are most important—honesty, respect, hard work—by sharing how these values have played out in their own lives. They can tell stories of times when honesty led to trust, when respect built strong relationships, and when hard work brought rewards that were worth the effort.

Grandparents also play a critical role in teaching children about resilience. Life isn't always easy, and no one knows that better than those who have lived through many seasons. Grandparents have faced loss, disappointment, and change, but they've also learned how to keep going, to find joy in new beginnings, and to hold on to hope even when things seem bleak. This resilience is a lesson that children need to learn, and who better to teach it than someone who has lived it?

But perhaps the most important thing grandparents offer is unconditional love. While parents are often caught up in the responsibilities of raising a child—setting rules, enforcing discipline, guiding behaviour—grandparents can offer love that isn't tied to performance or behaviour. They love simply because they do. This unconditional love provides a foundation of security that helps children feel valued just for being themselves.

Consider the way a grandparent looks at their grandchild. It's a look filled with pride, with joy, and with a deep love that says, "You are special to me, just as you are." This kind of love is a powerful force in a child's life. It gives them the confidence to explore the world, to try new things, and to become the person they're meant to be.

Grandparents also serve as a buffer during tough times. When family dynamics become strained, whether due to financial stress, illness, or other challenges, grandparents can provide a steady presence that helps to ease the tension. They offer a safe space for children to retreat to, a place where they can feel secure and loved, even when things are difficult at home. This role is invaluable, providing emotional support not just to the child, but to the entire family.

99

"To us, family means putting your arms around each other and being there."

In the end, the role of grandparents is irreplaceable. They bring wisdom that can only come from experience, warmth that makes children feel safe and loved, and a perspective that helps children understand the world in a deeper way. They pass down values that have been shaped over a lifetime, teaching children not just how to live, but how to live well. And in doing so, they leave a legacy that lasts long after they're gone.

So cherish the relationship your child has with their grandparents. Encourage it, nurture it, and recognize the unique role they play in your child's life. It's a relationship built on love, respect, and a deep connection to family that will shape your child's heart and mind in ways that will last a lifetime. Grandparents are more than just family—they are the pillars that support the emotional growth and well-being of the next generation.

Aligning Family Values: Create a unified family approach that reinforces core values and emotional bonds.

Aligning family values is like tuning a set of instruments before a concert. Each member plays a different role, but together, they create harmony. When a family shares common values, the whole is greater than the sum of its parts. The challenge is making sure everyone is on the same page, playing the same tune, and working towards the same goals.

Values are the guiding principles that shape our decisions, our behaviour, and our relationships. In a family, these values are passed down, not just through words, but through actions. They're what your children see when you make choices, how you treat others, and how you handle adversity. These values become the foundation of your family's identity, and they're essential for creating a strong emotional bond.

But how do you create a unified family approach that reinforces these core values? It starts with communication. The first step is to sit down as a family and talk about what's important. This isn't a onetime conversation, but an ongoing dialogue. Each member of the family should have a voice, even the youngest. Ask questions like, "What do we stand for as a family?" and "What kind of people do we want to be?" These questions help to bring out what matters most to each person.

Once you've identified your core values, the next step is to align your actions with them. It's one thing to say that honesty is important, but it's another to live it out every day. This means being truthful with each other, even when it's hard. It means owning up to mistakes and showing your children that honesty isn't just a rule—it's a way of life. When your actions match your words, you reinforce the values you want to instill.

Consistency is key. Values aren't something you can turn on and off. They should be woven into the fabric of your daily life. This means that the rules you set, the decisions you make, and the way you interact with each other should all reflect your family's values. If kindness is a core value, then it should show in how you speak to each other, how you handle disagreements, and how you treat those outside your family.

One powerful way to reinforce family values is through rituals and traditions. These are the repeated actions that give your family identity and meaning. It could be as simple as having dinner together every night, where you all share what you're grateful for. Or it could be a family volunteer day where you all give back to the community. These rituals don't just build bonds; they're a way to live out your values together.

But what happens when family members don't agree on certain values? This is where flexibility comes in. It's important to recognize that each person in the family is an individual with their own beliefs and experiences. The goal isn't to force everyone into the same mold, but to find common ground. If one person values independence while another values cooperation, talk about how these can coexist. Maybe independence is expressed in the way chores are done, while cooperation is highlighted in family decisions.

Respect is a cornerstone of aligning family values. Even when you disagree, it's crucial to respect each other's opinions and feelings. This shows your children that, while values are important, the way we treat each other matters just as much. If respect is a core value, it should be evident in every interaction. This means listening when someone speaks, avoiding harsh words, and valuing each person's perspective.

As children grow, their understanding of values deepens. What might start as simple rules, like "Always tell the truth," evolves into more complex ideas about integrity and trust. It's important to revisit these conversations as your children mature. Ask them how they see your family values playing out in their lives. Encourage them to think critically about what they believe and why. This helps them take ownership of the values, making them more likely to carry them into adulthood.

One challenge in aligning family values is dealing with outside influences. Friends, media, and society all have their own sets of values, which might not always align with yours. It's important to talk about these influences openly. If your child sees behaviour that conflicts with your family's values, discuss it. Ask them how they feel about it and what they think the right approach would be. This not only reinforces your family's values but also teaches critical thinking.

Modeling is another powerful tool. Children learn more from what you do than from what you say. If generosity is a family value, show it in your actions. Let your children see you helping others, giving your time, or sharing what you have. When they see these values lived out, they understand them on a deeper level. They see that values aren't just abstract ideas, but practical ways to live a meaningful life.

It's also important to celebrate when your family lives out its values. Acknowledge the moments when someone does something that reflects your core principles. It doesn't have to be a big deal—just a simple "I noticed how you helped your sister today, and that was really kind" can go a long way. These acknowledgments reinforce the idea that values are something to be proud of.

But aligning family values isn't just about the good times. It's also about how you handle challenges. Life isn't always easy, and it's in the tough moments that your values are truly tested. Whether it's a financial setback, a disagreement, or a loss, how your family responds says a lot about what you stand for. If your value is perseverance, show it by facing challenges head-on. If it's compassion, let it guide how you support each other through difficult times.

In the end, aligning family values is about creating a cohesive, supportive environment where each person feels valued and understood. It's about building a foundation that can withstand the storms of life, because it's grounded in shared principles. When your family is united by common values, you create a strong, lasting bond that gives each member the confidence to face the world, knowing they're supported by a family that stands for something meaningful.

By working together to define and live out your family's values, you're not just raising children—you're building a legacy. A legacy of love, respect, and integrity that will carry on long after the children have grown and started families of their own. This is the true power of aligning family values: it's a gift that keeps giving, shaping not just the present, but the future as well.

> **"You don't choose your family. They are God's gift to you, as you are to them."**

CHAPTER SIX

PHYSICAL AND EMOTIONAL GROWTH

Nutrition for Body and Soul: The link between proper nutrition and emotional stability, and how to integrate them into daily life.

The food we eat shapes more than our bodies—it shapes our minds, too. Proper nutrition isn't just about physical health; it's about emotional well-being. What we feed our children affects how they feel, think, and handle the world around them. When we nourish their bodies with the right foods, we're also feeding their souls, helping them grow into balanced, resilient individuals.

Start with the basics. Food is fuel. Just as you wouldn't put the wrong fuel in your car, you shouldn't feed your child junk and expect them to run smoothly. The brain needs nutrients to function well. A diet rich in fruits, vegetables, whole grains, and lean proteins provides the vitamins and minerals that keep the mind sharp and moods steady.

Take breakfast, for example. Skipping it, or eating something sugary, sets a rocky foundation for the day. A good breakfast— think eggs, whole-grain toast, and some fruit—gives the brain the steady energy it needs. It's like laying down a strong track for the train to run on, ensuring your child stays focused and calm.

But there's more to nutrition than just keeping blood sugar levels stable. The food we eat impacts brain chemistry, which influences how we feel. Omega-3 fatty acids, found in fish like salmon and in walnuts, play a significant role here. These fats help reduce inflammation in the brain, linked to depression and anxiety. Adding these foods to your child's diet can support a balanced mood and a clear mind.

Complex carbohydrates are another key player. Unlike the quick highs and crashes from sugary snacks, complex carbs provide a slow, steady release of glucose. This helps keep your child's mood on an even keel, avoiding the spikes and drops that can lead to irritability. Whole grains, beans, and vegetables are the go-to sources. These foods help maintain energy throughout the day, supporting both body and mind.

There's also the gut-brain connection to consider. The gut is often called the "second brain" because of its profound influence on mental health. A healthy gut, full of good bacteria, supports a healthy brain. This is where probiotics come in—foods like yogurt, kefir, and fermented vegetables such as sauerkraut or kimchi. These foods help maintain a balance of gut bacteria, which in turn supports emotional stability. A healthy gut can mean a happier child.

Hydration is another crucial element often overlooked. Dehydration can lead to fatigue, trouble focusing, and mood swings. Encourage your child to drink water throughout the day. A hydrated brain is a better-functioning brain, one that can handle stress and stay balanced.

But how do you make sure these nutritional principles become a regular part of daily life? The key is to make healthy eating simple and enjoyable, not a chore. Start by involving your child in the process. Let them help pick out fruits and vegetables at the store. Teach them how to prepare meals with you. When they're involved, they're more likely to enjoy the food and appreciate what it does for their body and mind.

Make healthy eating a family affair. Children learn by watching what you do, not just by hearing what you say. If they see you reaching for a piece of fruit instead of a bag of chips, they're more likely to do the same. Family meals are a perfect time to model these habits. Sitting down together to share a meal isn't just about eating; it's about connecting, discussing the day, and enjoying each other's company. This routine provides stability and teaches your child that healthy eating is a normal part of life.

You don't have to prepare elaborate meals to eat well. Keep it simple. A balanced plate with a protein source, a vegetable, and a whole grain is all you need. Snacks can be easy, too—apple slices with peanut butter, a handful of nuts, or some yogurt with berries. These options are nutritious, satisfying, and help keep energy levels steady throughout the day.

Breakfast, lunch, and dinner aren't the only opportunities to nourish your child. Snack time is another chance to provide their body and mind with what they need. Instead of processed snacks that offer little more than empty calories, opt for nutrient-dense choices. Fresh fruit, raw vegetables with hummus, or a smoothie with spinach, banana, and almond milk can do wonders for your child's mood and focus.

It's not just about what to eat but also about what to avoid. Processed foods, with their high sugar and unhealthy fats, can wreak havoc on both body and mind. They cause quick energy spikes followed by crashes, which can lead to mood swings, irritability, and trouble concentrating. Limiting these foods and focusing on whole natural options will help keep your child's energy and emotions stable.

Another powerful tool is consistency. The brain and body thrive on routine. Regular meal times, with balanced meals and snacks, help maintain steady energy and mood. This consistency provides a sense of security, helping your child feel more grounded and emotionally stable.

Sometimes, though, it's not just about the food itself but the environment in which it's eaten. Mealtime should be a time of calm, not stress. Avoid distractions like TV or phones during meals. Focus on enjoying the food and the company. This mindful approach to eating helps children connect with their food and their family, creating a positive association with mealtimes.

Finally, remember that food is just one piece of the puzzle. While proper nutrition is essential for physical and emotional health, it works best when combined with other healthy habits—regular exercise, plenty of sleep, and positive social interactions.

Together, these elements create a foundation for a balanced, healthy life.

> **99**
>
> *"Health is a state of complete harmony of the body, mind, and spirit. When one is free from physical disabilities and mental distractions, the gates of the soul open."*

In the end, feeding your child isn't just about filling their stomach; it's about nurturing their body, mind, and soul. By providing them with the right nutrients, you're giving them the tools they need to thrive, both physically and emotionally. It's an investment in their future, one meal at a time. So, take the time to choose foods that nourish their whole being. The benefits will be felt far beyond the dinner table, shaping their health, happiness, and resilience for years to come.

Moving Together: Physical Activities that Bond: Engage in activities that boost physical health and strengthen emotional ties.

Physical activity isn't just about keeping the body healthy; it's also a powerful way to connect with your child. Moving together strengthens more than just muscles—it builds bonds that last a lifetime. When you engage in activities as a family, you're not just promoting physical health; you're also nurturing emotional ties.

Start with something simple, like a walk. Walking might seem mundane, but it's one of the easiest ways to spend time together. It doesn't require special equipment or skills, just a good pair of shoes and a willingness to move. Take a walk around the neighborhood after dinner, or head to a nearby park on the weekends. As you walk, talk about your day, share stories, or simply enjoy the silence together. The rhythm of walking side by side creates a space for conversation, for bonding without the pressure of eye contact. It's a time to slow down, to connect without distractions, and to breathe in the world around you.

Then there's biking. Riding bikes together brings a sense of adventure. Whether it's a leisurely ride around the block or a more challenging trail, biking is a great way to explore new places and experience the joy of movement. When you ride together, you're teaching your child about balance, both physically and emotionally. The ups and downs of a bike ride mirror the ups and downs of life. Sometimes you pedal hard to get up a hill, and other times you coast down with the wind in your face. Sharing these experiences creates memories that stick, reinforcing the idea that life's challenges are easier to tackle together.

If you want something a bit more structured, try a family game of soccer, basketball, or even tag. These games are more than just fun—they teach teamwork, strategy, and fair play. When you play together, you're also leveling the playing field. It's not about who's the fastest or strongest; it's about enjoying the game and the time spent with each other. Playing sports together helps children learn to deal with winning and losing, to celebrate successes and bounce back from defeats. It's a way to practice resilience in a safe, supportive environment.

Swimming is another excellent activity that combines physical exercise with emotional bonding. The water offers a unique setting where movement feels different—lighter, freer. Whether you're teaching your child to swim or just splashing around in the pool, the water has a way of bringing out laughter and playfulness. Swimming together also encourages trust. In the water, your child looks to you for safety and guidance, and each successful swim strengthens their confidence and your bond.

Hiking is perfect for families who love the outdoors. It's an activity that challenges the body and soothes the soul. The beauty of nature provides a backdrop for deep conversations or quiet reflection. Hiking teaches endurance, patience, and the joy of reaching a goal together. Whether you're trekking up a mountain or walking through a wooded trail, the shared experience of navigating nature's paths brings you closer. Each step taken together, each view admired, builds a sense of accomplishment and connection.

For a more calming experience, consider yoga. Yoga isn't just about stretching or holding poses; it's about mindfulness and breathing. Practicing yoga as a family can help everyone slow down, center themselves, and connect on a deeper level. It teaches children to listen to their bodies, to focus on the present, and to find peace within. The gentle movements and shared focus create a peaceful space where everyone can unwind and recharge together.

Dance is another activity that brings families together. Whether it's a spontaneous dance party in the living room or a more structured dance class, moving to music is a joyful way to connect. Dancing allows for expression without words, for letting go and having fun. It's an activity that transcends age— whether you're twirling with a toddler or grooving with a teenager, the shared joy of dance brings smiles and laughter. Plus, it's a great way to burn off energy and relieve stress.

Gardening might not seem like a physical activity at first glance, but it's a wonderful way to get moving and bond with your child. Digging, planting, and weeding all require physical effort, and the rewards are visible. Gardening teaches patience and care, as you nurture plants together and watch them grow. It's also a time to talk, to share thoughts, and to work side by side on something that brings life and beauty. The quiet moments spent tending to a garden can be some of the most meaningful, as you connect not only with each other but with the earth.

Even chores can be turned into bonding activities. Raking leaves, washing the car, or even cleaning the house can become fun when done together. Turn on some music, make it a game, and suddenly, what might have been a boring task becomes a way to connect. Working together on chores teaches responsibility and teamwork, and the sense of accomplishment at the end of the day is something to be shared.

> **"**
>
> *"Physical fitness is not only one of the most important keys to a healthy body, it is the basis of dynamic and creative intellectual activity."*

But the key to all these activities is not the activity itself but the time spent together. The focus should be on the connection, not on perfecting the skill. Whether you're walking, biking, playing, or simply moving together, you're showing your child that they're worth your time and attention. You're creating a safe space where they can be themselves, where they know they're loved, and where they can grow both physically and emotionally.

In the end, it's the memories you create together that will last. The shared laughter, the challenges overcome, the quiet moments of reflection—these are the things your child will carry with them into adulthood. Moving together isn't just about exercise; it's about building a foundation of love, trust, and connection that will support your child throughout their life.

So, lace up your shoes, grab a ball, or roll out a yoga mat. Whatever activity you choose, do it together. Because when you move as a family, you're not just building stronger bodies; you're building stronger bonds. And that's the true power of physical activity—it's not just about staying healthy; it's about staying connected.

~~Creating a Holistic Environment: Build a nurturing~~ atmosphere that supports your child's overall well-being.

Creating a nurturing environment for your child is like planting a garden. You choose the soil, the seeds, and the sunlight to ensure that everything grows strong and healthy. A holistic environment does more than just support your child's physical needs—it fosters their emotional, mental, and social well-being as well.

Let's start with the physical space. The home is where your child spends most of their time, and it should be a place that feels safe and welcoming. Keep the living areas clean and uncluttered. A tidy space helps to clear the mind, making it easier for your child to focus and relax. Natural light is another important factor. Open the curtains during the day to let in as much sunlight as possible. Sunlight not only brightens the room but also boosts mood and energy levels.

Next, consider the colors and textures in your home. Soft, calming colors like blues and greens can create a soothing atmosphere. Think about the textures your child interacts with daily—plush rugs, soft pillows, and cozy blankets. These touches make a space feel comfortable and inviting, a place where your child can feel secure.

The sounds around your home also play a role in creating a holistic environment. Too much noise can be overstimulating, leading to stress and agitation. Instead, aim for a peaceful atmosphere. Play calming music in the background or embrace the quiet. Encourage a quiet time during the day where everyone can unwind—reading a book, listening to music, or simply sitting in silence. This helps your child learn the value of stillness and reflection.

A holistic environment also considers the food your child eats. As we discussed earlier, nutrition is closely tied to emotional and physical well-being. Stock your kitchen with healthy, whole foods that nourish the body and mind. Involve your child in meal planning and preparation, turning it into a learning experience. Teach them where their food comes from, how it's made, and why it's important to eat a balanced diet. This not only fosters healthy eating habits but also connects your child to the natural world.

Beyond physical health, a holistic environment nurtures emotional growth. This begins with the relationships within the home. Create an atmosphere of love and respect. Speak kindly to each other, listen without judgment, and resolve conflicts calmly. Children learn how to handle their emotions by watching how you handle yours. When they see you treating others with empathy and understanding, they learn to do the same.

Emotional security also comes from routine. Children thrive on predictability—it gives them a sense of control in a world that often feels overwhelming. Establish a daily routine that includes regular mealtimes, playtimes, and bedtime. Routines provide structure, helping your child know what to expect and reducing anxiety. They also create opportunities for connection, such as sharing a meal together or reading a bedtime story.

Encouraging creativity is another key part of a holistic environment. Provide your child with the tools to explore their imagination—crayons, paper, building blocks, or musical instruments. Creativity is more than just play; it's a way for your child to express their feelings, solve problems, and think critically. Offer them time and space to create without pressure, allowing their imagination to flourish.

Physical activity is crucial as well. Encourage movement throughout the day. This doesn't have to mean organized sports, although those are great too. It can be as simple as dancing in the living room, playing tag in the yard, or taking a family walk after dinner. Physical activity helps burn off energy, reduces stress, and promotes better sleep. Plus, it's a fun way to spend time together, strengthening both bodies and bonds.

Connecting with nature is another powerful way to build a holistic environment. Nature has a calming effect, helping to reduce stress and improve mood. Make time for outdoor activities—whether it's hiking, gardening, or just playing in the park. Teach your child to appreciate the beauty of the natural world and the importance of taking care of it. These experiences not only boost physical health but also foster a sense of wonder and respect for the environment.

Social connections are also a vital part of a holistic environment. Encourage your child to build relationships with friends and family. These connections provide support, companionship, and a sense of belonging. Arrange playdates, family gatherings, or community activities where your child can interact with others. Social skills are learned through experience, and these interactions teach your child how to communicate, cooperate, and resolve conflicts.

Lastly, a holistic environment supports mental well-being. Encourage your child to explore new ideas, ask questions, and seek out knowledge. Create a home that values learning—whether through books, educational games, or simply engaging in thoughtful conversations. Support their interests, whatever they may be, and provide the resources they need to explore them further. This not only stimulates their mind but also builds confidence and a lifelong love of learning.

But remember, a holistic environment isn't just about the things you do; it's about the energy you bring. Children are incredibly sensitive to the emotions of those around them. If you're stressed, anxious, or angry, they'll pick up on it. It's important to take care of your own well-being too. Practice self-care, find ways to manage stress, and approach parenting with patience and love. When you're calm and centered, you create a peaceful environment that benefits the whole family.

In the end, building a holistic environment is about creating a space where your child feels loved, safe, and free to grow. It's about nurturing their body, mind, and spirit in a way that supports their overall well-being. By paying attention to the physical space, fostering emotional connections, and encouraging creativity and exploration, you're giving your child the tools they need to thrive.

This environment doesn't have to be perfect—it just needs to be thoughtful and intentional. Every small change, every effort to create a more nurturing atmosphere, makes a difference. Over time, these efforts add up, creating a home where your child feels secure, happy, and ready to take on the world. And that's the true goal of a holistic environment: not just to raise a healthy child, but to raise a well-rounded, resilient individual who knows they are loved and capable, no matter what life brings.

99

"The energy of the mind is the essence of life."

CHAPTER SEVEN

MORAL AND SOCIAL LESSONS

Values that Shape Character: Teach the principles that will guide your child through life.

Teaching values is like planting seeds. You sow them early, tend to them carefully, and watch as they take root and grow into strong, guiding principles. These values shape your child's character, steering them through life's challenges and decisions. They are the moral compass that helps them find their way, even when the path isn't clear.

Start with honesty. It's the bedrock of trust and integrity. Teaching your child to be honest begins with your own example. Children are always watching, and they learn more from what you do than from what you say. Be truthful in your interactions, whether it's admitting when you've made a mistake or telling the truth, even when it's difficult. When your child sees you value honesty, they're more likely to do the same.

But honesty isn't just about telling the truth. It's also about being true to oneself. Encourage your child to express their thoughts and feelings openly, without fear of judgment. Let them know it's okay to say what they believe, even if it's not what others want to hear. This helps them build confidence in their own voice and teaches them the importance of being authentic.

Respect is another cornerstone of character. It's about treating others the way you want to be treated. This lesson starts at home, with how family members treat each other. Show respect in the way you talk to your child, your partner, and others. Simple acts like listening when someone is speaking, using polite language, and acknowledging others' feelings go a long way. When children see respect in action, they learn to give it in return.

Respect also extends to understanding differences. Teach your child to appreciate diversity, whether it's in opinions, cultures, or abilities. Encourage them to ask questions, to be curious about the world around them, and to see value in perspectives different from their own. This not only fosters respect but also broadens their understanding of the world and the people in it.

Kindness is another value that shapes character deeply. Acts of kindness, no matter how small, make a big impact. Encourage your child to look for ways to help others—holding the door open, offering a smile, or helping a friend in need. These actions teach them empathy and compassion. When they experience the positive effects of kindness, they'll understand its importance and carry it with them throughout their lives.

Teaching responsibility is crucial. Responsibility means being accountable for one's actions and understanding the consequences of those actions. Start with small tasks at home—chores, taking care of a pet, or managing homework. These responsibilities teach your child the importance of reliability and follow through. As they grow, these small lessons in responsibility will translate into larger ones, such as taking responsibility for their choices and their impact on others.

Perseverance is a value that will serve your child well in all aspects of life. Life is full of challenges, and the ability to keep going, even when things get tough, is essential. Encourage your child to stick with tasks, even when they're difficult. Praise their efforts, not just the outcomes. Let them know it's okay to fail, as long as they keep trying. Perseverance isn't about never failing; it's about never giving up.

Fairness is another principle that shapes character. Teach your child the importance of treating others fairly, of giving everyone a chance. This lesson starts in everyday situations—sharing toys, taking turns, or playing by the rules. When your child understands fairness, they learn about justice and equality. They learn that everyone deserves to be treated with respect and kindness, no matter who they are.

Gratitude is a value that can transform your child's outlook on life. Teach them to appreciate what they have, to be thankful for the small things as well as the big ones. Encourage them to express gratitude regularly—saying "thank you" when someone helps them, writing a note of thanks, or simply taking a moment each day to reflect on what they're grateful for. Gratitude helps children develop a positive mindset and reminds them to focus on the good in their lives.

Courage is another vital value. It's about doing what's right, even when it's hard. Teach your child to stand up for what they believe in, to face their fears, and to take risks when necessary. Courage isn't about being fearless; it's about facing fear and moving forward, anyway. Encourage them to take small steps outside their comfort zone, to try new things, and to speak up when something doesn't feel right. These experiences build their confidence and their character.

Generosity is a value that enriches both the giver and the receiver. Teach your child the joy of giving, whether it's sharing their time, their talents, or their resources. Encourage them to volunteer, to help a friend, or to donate to those in need. Generosity teaches children that they have the power to make a difference in the world, and that giving is often more rewarding than receiving.

Finally, humility is a value that keeps us grounded. Teach your child that it's important to be proud of their achievements, but also to recognize the contributions of others. Encourage them to celebrate their successes, but to remain modest and gracious. Humility helps them build strong, respectful relationships and reminds them that everyone has something to offer.

In the end, teaching values is about more than just words—it's about living those values every day. It's about creating an environment where honesty, respect, kindness, responsibility, perseverance, fairness, gratitude, courage, generosity, and humility are not just taught, but practiced. It's about showing your child that these values are not just principles to follow, but the foundation of a good life.

> *"The best way to find yourself is to lose yourself in the service of others."*

By instilling these values in your child, you're giving them the tools they need to navigate the world with integrity, compassion, and confidence. You're helping them build a character that will guide them through life's challenges and joys, and that will serve them well, no matter where life takes them. And that's the greatest gift you can give them—a strong moral compass that will always point them in the right direction.

The Family's Role in Socialization: How your family environment influences your child's social development.

The family is the first school your child ever attends. Long before they step into a classroom or playground, they learn from you—their first teacher. The way you interact with them, the way you treat others, and the environment you create at home all play a crucial role in shaping how they navigate the social world.

Socialization begins at home. The family is the primary influence in your child's early years. It's where they learn how to communicate, how to behave, and how to interact with others. From the moment they're born, your child is observing, absorbing, and mimicking. They watch how you talk, how you solve problems, and how you handle emotions. These early lessons form the foundation for their social development.

Communication is at the heart of socialization. The way you speak to your child teaches them how to express themselves. If you communicate with kindness and patience, your child learns to do the same. If you listen when they talk, they learn that their voice matters and that communication is a two-way street. Encourage open dialogue at home. Ask your child about their day, listen to their stories, and validate their feelings. This helps them develop the confidence to express themselves clearly and respectfully in the wider world.

The family environment also teaches your child about relationships. How you and your partner interact, how you resolve conflicts, and how you show affection all serve as models for your child. They learn about love, trust, and respect by watching how you treat each other. If your home is filled with warmth, understanding, and support, your child learns that these are the foundations of healthy relationships. They carry these lessons with them as they form friendships and other relationships outside the family.

But socialization isn't just about learning how to talk and interact; it's also about understanding social norms and values. Your family's values become your child's guide to what's right and wrong, what's important, and what's expected of them in society. If honesty is a core value in your home, your child learns that truthfulness is important. If respect is emphasized, they learn to treat others with consideration. These values shape how they behave in social situations, how they respond to others, and how they see themselves in relation to the world.

Routines and traditions also play a role in socialization. Family meals, holiday celebrations, and daily rituals provide a sense of stability and belonging. These shared experiences help your child feel connected to something bigger than themselves. They learn the importance of being part of a community, of contributing to family life, and of respecting shared customs. This sense of belonging and tradition gives them the confidence to participate in social activities outside the home, knowing they have a strong foundation to fall back on.

Socialization also involves teaching your child how to navigate social hierarchies and authority. The way you handle rules and discipline at home sets the stage for how your child will interact with authority figures, such as teachers or coaches, later on. Clear, consistent boundaries teach them about respect for rules and the importance of following guidelines. However, it's equally important to teach them how to question authority respectfully, to think critically, and to stand up for what they believe in. This balance helps them develop into socially adept and independent thinkers.

Conflict resolution is another key aspect of socialization. Disagreements are inevitable, both within the family and in the outside world. How you handle conflicts at home teaches your child how to approach disagreements in a healthy way. If they see you resolving conflicts through calm discussion and compromise, they'll learn that arguments don't have to lead to fights, that it's possible to disagree without being disagreeable. Encourage your child to talk about their feelings, to listen to others, and to find solutions that work for everyone involved.

The family's role in socialization also extends to teaching empathy. Empathy is the ability to understand and share the feelings of others, and it's a crucial skill for successful social interactions. You can nurture empathy in your child by modeling it yourself—by showing kindness, by helping others, and by discussing feelings openly. When your child sees you considering how your actions affect others, they learn to do the same. Encourage them to think about how others might feel in different situations and to respond with kindness and understanding.

Peer interactions within the family, especially with siblings, also play a big role in socialization. Siblings provide a built-in social network where children can practice sharing, cooperation, and conflict resolution. They learn how to navigate jealousy, competition, and the ups and downs of close relationships. While sibling rivalry is common, it's also a valuable learning experience. Encourage positive interactions between siblings, but also allow them to work through their disagreements. These interactions teach them important social skills that will serve them well in their friendships and other relationships.

Finally, it's important to remember that socialization is not just about teaching your child how to fit into society; it's also about helping them develop a strong sense of self. Encourage them to explore their interests, to express their individuality, and to be proud of who they are. A strong self-concept is essential for healthy social development. When children know who they are and what they stand for, they're better equipped to navigate social pressures and to form meaningful, respectful relationships.

> *"The principal goal of education in the schools should be creating men and women who are capable of doing new things, not simply repeating what other generations have done."*

In conclusion, the family's role in socialization is about more than just preparing your child to interact with others; it's about shaping who they become. The lessons they learn at home about communication, relationships, values, and empathy form the foundation for their social life. By creating a nurturing, supportive environment and modeling the behaviours you want to see, you're setting your child up for success in all their social interactions. These early lessons will stay with them, guiding them through the complexities of the social world, and helping them build a life filled with meaningful connections and positive relationships.

Raising Empathetic Children: Instill empathy and compassion through consistent emotional support and modeling.

Raising empathetic children is like planting seeds in a garden. You nurture them with care, attention, and love, and over time, they grow into compassionate, understanding individuals. Empathy doesn't just happen; it's cultivated through consistent emotional support and by modeling the behaviours you want to see in your child.

Empathy begins at home. From the moment your child is born, they start to learn about emotions—first their own, and then the emotions of those around them. As they grow, they begin to understand that other people have feelings too. But understanding isn't enough. They need to learn how to connect with those feelings, to put themselves in someone else's shoes, and to respond with kindness and care.

The first step in teaching empathy is to create an emotionally supportive environment. This means making your home a safe space where feelings are acknowledged and respected. When your child expresses their emotions, whether they're happy, sad, or angry, take the time to listen. Validate their feelings by saying things like, "I can see that you're upset," or "That must have made you really happy." This shows your child that their emotions matter and that it's okay to express them.

But empathy isn't just about recognizing and understanding emotions; it's also about responding to them in a compassionate way. When your child sees you responding to their feelings with empathy, they learn to do the same with others. For example, if your child is upset because a toy broke, instead of just fixing it or replacing it, take a moment to acknowledge their disappointment. Say something like, "I'm sorry that your toy broke. I know you really liked it." This helps them feel understood and teaches them to consider how others might feel in similar situations.

Modeling empathy is one of the most powerful ways to teach it. Children learn by watching the adults in their lives. When you show empathy in your interactions with others, your child is likely to follow your lead. If someone in your life is going through a tough time, talk to your child about it. Explain why you're sending a card, making a phone call, or offering help. Let them see you being kind and compassionate. This shows them that empathy is not just a feeling, but something you act on.

Another important aspect of raising empathetic children is teaching them to recognize the impact of their actions on others. When they do something that affects someone else, talk to them about it. For instance, if they hurt a friend's feelings, instead of simply telling them to apologize, help them understand why the friend is upset. Ask them, "How do you think they felt when that happened?" This encourages them to think beyond their own perspective and to consider the feelings of others.

Books and stories are also powerful tools for teaching empathy. When you read together, choose stories that explore different emotions and experiences. As you read, ask your child questions like, "How do you think the character feels?" or "What would you do in that situation?" These discussions help your child practice putting themselves in someone else's shoes. They also introduce them to a wide range of emotions and situations, broadening their understanding of others.

Encouraging your child to help others is another way to build empathy. This could be as simple as helping a sibling with homework or as involved as participating in community service. When children see the positive impact their actions can have on others, it reinforces the value of kindness and compassion. It also gives them a sense of responsibility for the well-being of others, which is a key component of empathy.

Friendships are a natural arena for practicing empathy. As your child forms relationships with peers, they'll encounter situations that require understanding and compassion. Be there to guide them through these interactions. If they come to you with a problem involving a friend, listen carefully, and offer advice on how to approach the situation with empathy. Encourage them to talk to their friend, to listen to their side of the story, and to find a solution that considers both of their feelings.

However, it's important to remember that empathy also involves setting boundaries. Teach your child that while it's important to care for others, they also need to take care of themselves. Empathy shouldn't come at the expense of their own well-being. Help them understand that it's okay to say no, to take a step back when they need to, and to ask for help when they're overwhelmed. This balance is crucial for developing healthy, sustainable empathy.

Another aspect of empathy is learning to deal with differences. The world is full of people with different backgrounds, beliefs, and experiences. Teach your child to appreciate these differences and to approach them with an open mind. Encourage them to ask questions, to learn about other cultures, and to understand that everyone has their own story. This not only broadens their perspective but also helps them connect with people who are different from them.

Empathy also involves forgiveness. Teach your child that everyone makes mistakes, and that it's important to forgive others when they do. This doesn't mean excusing bad behaviour, but rather understanding that people are imperfect and that holding onto anger doesn't help anyone. Encourage your child to talk about their feelings when they've been hurt, and to work through those feelings in a healthy way. This helps them develop the emotional resilience needed to maintain compassionate relationships.

Finally, celebrate empathy when you see it. When your child shows kindness, understanding, or compassion, acknowledge it. Let them know that you noticed their empathetic behaviour and that you're proud of them. Positive reinforcement encourages them to continue practicing empathy and shows them that these actions are valued.

In the end, raising empathetic children is about more than just teaching them to be nice. It's about helping them understand the importance of caring for others, of connecting with people on a deeper level, and of acting with compassion in a world that often needs it. By providing consistent emotional support and modeling empathetic behaviour, you're giving your child the tools they need to build strong, meaningful relationships and to make a positive impact on the world around them.

These lessons in empathy will serve them well throughout their lives. They'll help them navigate the complexities of relationships, build stronger communities, and contribute to a more compassionate world. And as they grow, they'll carry these values with them, passing them on to the next generation, and continuing the cycle of empathy and compassion that you started.

> "Example is not the main thing in influencing others. It is the only thing."

CHAPTER EIGHT

CULTURE AND EMOTION

The Indian Family's Emotional Landscape: Explore the cultural aspects of emotional parenting within Indian families.

The Indian family is a unique tapestry woven with threads of tradition, love, respect, and a deep sense of togetherness. At the heart of this intricate design lies a distinct approach to emotional parenting, shaped by centuries of cultural practices, values, and beliefs. Understanding this emotional landscape offers insight into how Indian families nurture their children, instill values, and build strong emotional bonds.

In Indian families, emotions are not just individual experiences but are closely tied to the collective well-being of the family unit. The family is often viewed as a single entity, where each member's emotions and actions influence the entire group. This interconnectedness fosters a sense of responsibility towards one another, where the happiness or distress of one member is felt by all. This shared emotional experience is a cornerstone of Indian family life.

Respect is a key value in the emotional fabric of Indian families. Children are taught from a young age to respect their elders, not just in their actions but in their emotions as well. This respect is demonstrated through listening to elders, valuing their opinions, and considering their feelings in decision-making. Elders, in turn, reciprocate this respect by offering guidance, wisdom, and emotional support. This mutual respect creates a strong foundation of trust and understanding within the family.

Emotional expression in Indian families is often nuanced and varies depending on the situation and the relationship between family members. For instance, parents may express love and care through actions rather than words. Cooking a favorite meal, ensuring the child is well-prepared for school, or arranging family gatherings are ways parents show their affection. These acts of service are deeply rooted in the belief that love is best expressed through care and responsibility.

The extended family plays a significant role in the emotional development of children in India. Grandparents, uncles, aunts, and cousins are often actively involved in a child's upbringing, providing additional layers of emotional support and guidance. This involvement creates a broad emotional network where children learn from multiple role models. The presence of extended family members also ensures that children grow up with a strong sense of belonging and security.

Indian families often prioritize collective goals over individual desires, a value that is instilled in children from an early age. Sacrifice for the greater good of the family is a common theme, where personal ambitions may be set aside for the benefit of the family unit. This sense of duty and responsibility towards the family teaches children the importance of empathy, selflessness, and consideration for others.

Cultural practices and rituals also play a vital role in shaping the emotional landscape of Indian families. Festivals, religious ceremonies, and family traditions are opportunities for families to come together, reinforcing emotional bonds and shared values. These rituals provide a sense of continuity and stability, reminding children of their roots and the importance of family unity.

Communication in Indian families can sometimes be indirect, especially when it comes to expressing negative emotions like anger or disappointment. Parents might use non-verbal cues or indirect language to convey their feelings, expecting children to understand and respond accordingly. This subtle form of communication teaches children to be sensitive to the emotions of others, to read between the lines, and to respond with empathy and respect.

However, the emotional landscape of Indian families is not without its challenges. The emphasis on respect for elders and collective well-being can sometimes lead to the suppression of individual emotions and desires. Children might feel pressured to conform to family expectations, even if it conflicts with their personal feelings or aspirations. This can lead to internal conflicts and emotional stress if not addressed with care and understanding.

The changing dynamics of Indian society, with increasing urbanization and exposure to global cultures, are also influencing the emotional landscape of families. Younger generations are beginning to adopt more open and direct forms of communication, expressing their emotions more freely. This shift is leading to a blend of traditional values with modern approaches to emotional expression, creating a more diverse and dynamic emotional environment within families.

Balancing these traditional values with the needs of modern life requires flexibility and open-mindedness. Parents need to find ways to honor cultural traditions while also allowing their children the freedom to express themselves and pursue their own paths. This balance can be achieved through open communication, mutual respect, and a willingness to adapt to changing circumstances.

The role of women in the emotional landscape of Indian families is also significant. Mothers, in particular, are often seen as the emotional anchors of the family, responsible for maintaining harmony and ensuring the well-being of all members. Their influence on the emotional development of children is profound as they model behaviours of care, sacrifice, and emotional resilience. However, this role can also place a heavy burden on women, who may feel the pressure to suppress their own emotions to meet the needs of the family.

To foster a healthy emotional environment, it's important for Indian families to create spaces where all members feel valued and heard. This includes encouraging open dialogue, allowing children to express their emotions without fear of judgment, and recognizing the individual needs and aspirations of each family member. By doing so, families can nurture emotional well-being while still honoring the rich cultural traditions that define Indian family life.

> **"We don't stop playing because we grow old; we grow old because we stop playing."**

In conclusion, the emotional landscape of Indian families is a complex and beautiful blend of tradition, respect, and collective well-being. While deeply rooted in cultural practices, it is also evolving to meet the needs of modern life. By understanding and navigating this landscape with care, families can continue to build strong emotional bonds that support the growth and happiness of every member. This approach not only preserves the richness of Indian culture but also ensures that children grow up with the emotional tools they need to thrive in a changing world.

Traditions that Teach: Use cultural rituals to reinforce emotional health and moral values.

Cultural traditions are the backbone of many families, especially in India, where rituals and customs are intertwined deeply with daily life. These traditions do more than preserve history—they serve as powerful tools for teaching emotional health and moral values. When woven into the fabric of family life, these rituals reinforce the principles that guide us, offering lessons that words alone can't always convey.

Take, for instance, the tradition of celebrating festivals. In India, festivals like Diwali, Eid, and Christmas are not just about lights, gifts, or feasts. They're about coming together as a family, sharing joy, and spreading kindness. During Diwali, the festival of lights, families clean their homes, light oil lamps, and share sweets with neighbors. But beneath the surface, these actions carry deeper meanings. The cleaning symbolizes letting go of negativity, while the lamps represent hope and the triumph of good over evil. By participating in these rituals, children learn about renewal, positivity, and the importance of fostering light in their own lives and the lives of others.

Family meals are another tradition rich with lessons. In many Indian households, eating together is a cherished practice, one that goes beyond simply sharing food. It's a time for connection, for listening and learning from one another. The act of serving food to others before taking your own portion teaches humility and selflessness. The conversations that flow around the table are opportunities to discuss values, share experiences, and offer guidance. These meals, whether they're daily dinners or special holiday feasts, reinforce the idea that family is a source of support and that everyone's voice matters.

Religious rituals also play a significant role in teaching values and emotional resilience. Morning prayers, lighting incense, or visiting temples are more than just spiritual acts—they're moments of reflection and gratitude. For example, the practice of offering prayers before starting the day instills a sense of purpose and grounding. It teaches children to begin their day with mindfulness, to recognize the blessings in their lives, and to approach challenges with a calm, centered mind. This ritual of reflection can be a powerful tool in teaching children to manage stress and maintain emotional balance.

Another tradition that carries deep emotional lessons is the celebration of rites of passage. In Indian culture, events like a child's first haircut, their coming-of-age ceremonies, or weddings are steeped in meaning. These milestones are celebrated with rituals that honor the transition from one stage of life to another. For instance, the Upanayana ceremony, often referred to as the "sacred thread ceremony," marks the entry into adulthood for Hindu boys. It's a day filled with rituals that symbolize the taking one of responsibilities and the pursuit of knowledge. Through such ceremonies, children learn about responsibility, respect for tradition, and the importance of community.

Even everyday rituals, like touching the feet of elders for blessings, carry emotional significance. This simple gesture teaches respect and gratitude, reminding children of the wisdom and love that elders offer. It's a tradition that reinforces the value of humility, of recognizing that we are part of something larger than ourselves, and that we stand on the shoulders of those who came before us.

Family storytelling is another powerful tradition that teaches emotional health and moral values. Stories passed down through generations carry the wisdom of ancestors and the moral lessons of old. Whether it's tales from the Mahabharata, stories of the Prophet Muhammad's kindness, or parables from the Bible, these narratives offer more than entertainment. They provide a framework for understanding right and wrong, for navigating life's challenges, and for building character. When parents and grandparents share these stories, they're not just preserving culture—they're planting seeds of empathy, courage, and integrity in the hearts of children.

Celebrations of harvest festivals, like Pongal in Tamil Nadu or Makar Sankranti in northern India, also offer lessons in gratitude and the importance of community. These festivals are times when families come together to thank the earth for its bounty. The rituals involved—such as cooking the first rice of the season or flying kites—teach children to appreciate nature, to be thankful for what they have, and to celebrate life's simple joys. These festivals also reinforce the idea that life is interconnected, that we rely on each other and the earth for our well-being.

In addition to these specific traditions, the overarching cultural practice of respecting elders teaches children about the importance of relationships. In many Indian families, the opinions and guidance of elders are given significant weight. This respect is not just about obedience; it's about valuing the experience and wisdom that elders bring. When children see their parents consulting grandparents or deferring to their judgment, they learn the importance of humility, of seeking counsel, and of honoring the contributions of those who have walked the path before them.

However, it's important to recognize that traditions should evolve to stay relevant. While it's crucial to preserve cultural practices, it's equally important to adapt them to the changing needs of families. This might mean explaining the meanings behind rituals to children, ensuring they understand why these traditions matter. It could also mean creating new rituals that align with the family's values, ensuring that the lessons of the past continue to guide future generations.

For example, a family might start a new tradition of volunteering together during festivals, extending the lessons of compassion and community service. Or they might create a weekly ritual of reflection, where each family member shares something they're grateful for or a lesson they've learned that week. These modern adaptations keep the spirit of tradition alive while making it relevant to today's world.

> *"There is no culture without a struggle. Culture is the spirit and the way of life, and it lives through how we interact with each other."*

In conclusion, cultural traditions are not just relics of the past; they are living practices that shape the emotional and moral landscape of children. By engaging in these rituals with intention and understanding, families can reinforce the values that matter most, teaching children to live with empathy, integrity, and a deep respect for their heritage. These traditions, whether ancient or newly created, are the threads that connect generations, weaving a tapestry of love, respect, and shared wisdom that supports the emotional health and moral strength of each family member.

Stories that Shape Values: The power of storytelling in imparting life lessons and emotional intelligence.

Storytelling is an ancient art, passed down from generation to generation, weaving wisdom into the fabric of our lives. In every culture, stories have been used not just to entertain, but to teach, to inspire, and to shape the values of the young. The tales we share with our children do more than fill their imaginations— they build their character, guide their moral compass, and nurture their emotional intelligence.

From the bedtime fables told in hushed tones to the grand epics recited during family gatherings, stories are powerful tools in teaching life's most important lessons. They offer children a safe space to explore complex emotions, understand the consequences of actions, and learn about the world around them. A story's characters become mirrors, reflecting the struggles and triumphs that children themselves will face.

Consider the timeless stories from the Panchatantra. These ancient Indian fables, with their clever animals and simple yet profound morals, have been teaching children for centuries. Each tale ends with a lesson that is both clear and subtle, easy for a child to grasp but rich enough to grow with them. The story of "The Monkey and the Crocodile," for instance, teaches about friendship, trust, and betrayal. When the monkey outwits the crocodile to save his life, children learn about the importance of quick thinking and caution in the face of danger. These lessons are wrapped in a narrative that is engaging and memorable, ensuring that the values stick long after the story ends.

Stories also serve as a bridge between generations, connecting children to the wisdom of their ancestors. When grandparents share tales from their youth or recount stories passed down to them, they are not just telling a story—they are passing on a legacy. These narratives become a part of the child's identity, grounding them in their heritage while teaching them the values that have sustained their family for generations.

Take, for example, the Mahabharata, one of India's greatest epics. It's a story filled with complex characters, moral dilemmas, and profound teachings. The tale of Arjuna on the battlefield, unsure of his duty, and his guidance from Krishna, offers deep lessons on duty, righteousness, and the struggle between good and evil. Children who hear these stories are not just learning about ancient heroes; they're absorbing the principles of courage, honor, and moral integrity.

But the power of storytelling isn't limited to epic tales and ancient fables. Everyday stories—those from your own life, or even fictional tales created on the spot—can be just as impactful. When you share a story about a challenge you overcame, your child learns about resilience and perseverance. When you tell them a tale about kindness you witnessed, they learn the value of compassion. These stories don't need to be grand or elaborate; they just need to be real and meaningful.

For younger children, simple stories about animals or everyday scenarios can teach important lessons in empathy and emotional understanding. A story about a dog who feels lonely when his friend leaves can help a child understand their own feelings of loneliness. By seeing the world through the eyes of the story's characters, children learn to recognize and articulate their own emotions, as well as those of others.

In addition to teaching values, stories also play a crucial role in developing emotional intelligence. Through stories, children encounter a wide range of emotions—happiness, sadness, fear, anger, and more. They see how characters navigate these feelings, how they make decisions, and how they deal with the consequences of their actions. This helps children understand their own emotions and develop the skills needed to manage them.

Moreover, stories allow children to experience difficult situations in a safe and controlled way. A story about a child dealing with the loss of a pet, for example, can prepare a young listener for similar experiences in their own life. They learn that it's okay to feel sad, that it's okay to cry, and that it's possible to heal. These narratives offer comfort and guidance, helping children navigate the emotional landscape of their lives.

But storytelling is not just a passive experience. Engaging children in the storytelling process—asking them to predict what happens next, to describe how they think a character feels, or to come up with their own endings—deepens their understanding and makes the lessons more personal. It also encourages creativity, critical thinking, and problem-solving skills.

Another powerful aspect of storytelling is its ability to address moral dilemmas in a way that feels natural and non-confrontational. Stories present situations where characters face difficult choices, allowing children to think about what they would do in the same situation. This helps them develop a sense of right and wrong, not through direct instruction, but through thoughtful consideration and discussion.

For instance, the story of "The Boy Who Cried Wolf" teaches about the consequences of lying. But beyond the simple moral, it opens up a discussion about trust, honesty, and the importance of being reliable. These conversations, sparked by stories, are crucial in helping children internalize the values that will guide them through life.

In many ways, storytelling is a form of indirect teaching. It doesn't lecture or impose; instead, it invites children to explore, to question, and to discover. The lessons learned through stories are often more impactful than those delivered through direct instruction because they engage the heart as well as the mind. A story that moves a child, that makes them laugh, cry, or think deeply, is a story that will stay with them, shaping their values and their understanding of the world.

As children grow, the stories they need evolve too. What resonates with a five-year-old might not have the same impact on a teenager. This is where the richness of storytelling comes in—there are stories for every age, every stage of development, and every lesson that needs to be learned. As parents and educators, our role is to choose stories that reflect the values we want to impart, and to present them in a way that speaks to the hearts and minds of our children.

In conclusion, stories are more than just entertainment—they are powerful tools for teaching values and developing emotional intelligence. Whether through ancient epics, family tales, or simple fables, storytelling offers children a way to explore complex emotions, understand moral principles, and learn about the world in a way that is both engaging and memorable. By making storytelling a regular part of your child's life, you are not just passing on knowledge—you are shaping the very foundation of their character.

"All our dreams can come true, if we have the courage to pursue them."

CHAPTER NINE

OVERCOMING PARENTING CHALLENGES

Understanding and Resolving Emotional Conflicts: Strategies for managing emotional misunderstandings and challenges.

Emotional conflicts in a family are as natural as the changing seasons. They arise from misunderstandings, unmet expectations, or simply the clashing of different perspectives. But while conflicts are inevitable, they don't have to be destructive. With the right strategies, they can become opportunities for growth, understanding, and stronger relationships.

First, it's essential to recognize that emotional conflicts often stem from unmet needs or unexpressed feelings. When emotions run high, it's easy for misunderstandings to escalate. The key to resolving these conflicts lies in understanding what's really going on beneath the surface. Is your child upset because they feel unheard? Is there a fear or insecurity driving their behaviour? By asking these questions, you begin to address the root of the conflict rather than just the symptoms.

Listening is your most powerful tool in these situations. But it's not just about hearing the words; it's about understanding the feelings behind them. When your child comes to you upset, resist the urge to jump in with solutions right away. Instead, give them the space to express themselves fully. Nodding, maintaining eye contact, and offering simple acknowledgments like "I see" or "I understand" can help them feel heard. Sometimes, all it takes to resolve a conflict is the reassurance that their emotions are valid and that you're there to support them.

However, simply listening isn't enough. After your child has expressed their feelings, it's important to reflect back on what you've heard to ensure you understand them correctly. For example, you might say, "It sounds like you're really frustrated because you feel like I'm not listening to you." This not only shows that you're paying attention but also gives your child a chance to clarify or correct any misunderstandings.

Empathy is another crucial element in resolving emotional conflicts. Put yourself in your child's shoes and try to see the situation from their perspective. How would you feel if you were in their position? Express this empathy verbally: "I can imagine how hard that must have been for you." This simple acknowledgment can go a long way in diffusing tension and building trust.

Once emotions have been acknowledged and understood, it's time to work together to find a solution. Involve your child in this process. Ask them what they think might help resolve the issue. This not only empowers them but also teaches problem-solving skills. If your child feels part of the solution, they're more likely to accept it and work towards it.

Setting clear boundaries is also vital. Emotional conflicts often arise when boundaries are unclear or not respected. Establishing and maintaining boundaries helps everyone in the family understand what is acceptable and what isn't. Be consistent with these boundaries, but also be willing to adjust them as your child grows and their needs change. Clear boundaries provide a sense of security, which can reduce the frequency and intensity of conflicts.

Communication should be open, honest, and respectful. Avoid raising your voice or using harsh words, as this can escalate the conflict. Instead, speak calmly and clearly, focusing on the issue at hand rather than past grievances or unrelated frustrations. If you feel yourself getting angry, take a moment to breathe and collect your thoughts before responding. Teaching your child to do the same can help them learn to manage their own emotions more effectively.

Another strategy is to use "I" statements rather than "you" statements. For example, instead of saying, "You never listen to me," you could say, "I feel frustrated when I don't feel heard." This approach focuses on your own feelings rather than placing blame, which can help prevent the other person from becoming defensive. It also encourages everyone involved to take responsibility for their own emotions and actions.

It's also important to recognize when to take a break. If a conflict is getting too heated, it might be best to step away for a little while and come back to it later. This gives everyone a chance to cool down and approach the issue with a clearer mind. Let your child know that it's okay to take a break if they're feeling overwhelmed and that you'll revisit the conversation when everyone is ready.

In some cases, emotional conflicts can bring up deep-seated issues that require more time and attention to resolve. If a particular conflict keeps recurring, it might be helpful to dig deeper into the underlying causes. This could involve talking to your child about their feelings over several conversations or seeking the help of a counselor if needed. Remember that some conflicts can't be resolved in a single conversation, and that's okay. What's important is to keep the lines of communication open and to approach the situation with patience and understanding.

Celebrating progress, no matter how small, is another way to encourage positive change. When a conflict is resolved, acknowledge the effort that went into finding a solution. Praise your child for their willingness to express their feelings, to listen, and to work towards a resolution. This reinforces the idea that conflicts can be managed in a healthy way and that everyone in the family plays a role in maintaining harmony.

Lastly, reflect on the conflict together after it's been resolved. Discuss what worked, what didn't, and how similar situations could be handled in the future. This reflection helps solidify the lessons learned and prepares both you and your child for future challenges. It's an opportunity to strengthen your relationship and to build the emotional resilience needed to face life's inevitable ups and downs.

In the end, emotional conflicts are a natural part of family life. They offer valuable opportunities for growth, both for you and your child. By approaching conflicts with empathy, patience, and a commitment to understanding, you can turn these challenges into moments of connection and learning. The strategies you used to resolve conflicts today will help your child develop the emotional intelligence they need to navigate relationships throughout their life. And in the process, you'll create a home environment where everyone feels heard, respected, and valued.

> **"When we are no longer able to change a situation, we are challenged to change ourselves."**

Balancing Work and Family: Practical advice on maintaining emotional connections while juggling responsibilities.

Balancing work and family is like walking a tightrope. You need to keep moving forward while staying steady, with each step carefully measured. In today's fast-paced world, where responsibilities pile up like bricks, maintaining emotional connections with your family can feel like a juggling act. But it's not impossible. With practical strategies and a mindful approach, you can ensure that your family stays close-knit, even as you manage the demands of work.

Start by setting clear priorities. Work is important—it provides for the family, gives you purpose, and allows you to grow. But your family is the reason you work so hard in the first place. Recognize that while work can be all-consuming, it shouldn't overshadow the time and emotional energy you invest in your loved ones. Make a conscious decision about what comes first. When you prioritize family, you make choices that reflect that decision, like setting boundaries around work hours or being fully present during family time.

Creating a schedule that respects both your work and family life is key. This doesn't mean rigidly compartmentalizing every hour of your day, but rather finding a rhythm that works for everyone. If possible, establish a set time each day for family activities—whether it's dinner together, a bedtime story, or a morning walk. These routines become anchors in your day, times when your family knows they have your full attention. Protect these moments like you would a crucial work meeting; they are just as important, if not more so.

When it comes to work, be mindful of how much time and energy you're giving it. The lines between work and home life can easily blur, especially if you work from home. To maintain balance, set clear boundaries. For example, once your workday is over, shut down your computer and put your phone away. Resist the temptation to check emails or finish one last task. By creating a physical and mental separation between work and home, you allow yourself to transition into family mode, where your focus is on the people who matter most.

Communication plays a vital role in balancing work and family. Be open with your family about your work commitments and let them know when you'll be especially busy. This transparency helps manage expectations and reduces misunderstandings. At the same time, encourage your family to share their needs and feelings with you. If your child feels like they're not getting enough of your attention, or your partner needs help with household responsibilities, knowing this allows you to make adjustments. Regular check-ins with your family can help keep everyone on the same page.

Quality over quantity is a principle that's especially important when balancing work and family. You may not always have as much time as you'd like with your loved ones, but the time you do have can be meaningful and impactful. Make the most of it by being fully present. When you're with your family, put away distractions. Listen to your child's stories, engage in activities together, and show interest in what they care about. These moments of connection, even if brief, strengthen emotional bonds and make your family feel valued.

Sometimes, the demands of work can make it hard to be physically present. When this happens, finding small ways to stay connected can make a big difference. A quick phone call or text message during the day to check in, a note in your child's lunchbox, or planning a special outing for the weekend can remind your family that they're always on your mind. These gestures show that you care, even when you're not there.

Delegating tasks at work and home is another practical way to balance responsibilities. At work, don't be afraid to ask for help or delegate tasks that don't require your direct involvement. This not only frees up your time but also helps you focus on the most important aspects of your job. At home, involve your family in household chores. Sharing responsibilities teaches children valuable life skills and lightens your load, giving you more time and energy to spend together.

Flexibility is key to balancing work and family. There will be days when work demands more of your time and others when family needs take precedence. Being adaptable and not rigid in your approach allows you to handle these fluctuations without guilt or stress. If you miss a family dinner because of work, make it up with a special breakfast the next day. If you need to take time off to care for a sick child, don't dwell on the work you're missing. Instead, focus on the opportunity to be there for your family when they need you most.

Self-care is another crucial aspect of maintaining balance. It's easy to get caught up in the demands of work and family, leaving little time for yourself. But neglecting your own needs can lead to burnout, making it harder to be present and effective in both areas of your life. Take time to recharge, whether it's through exercise, reading, or simply taking a few moments of quiet each day. When you take care of yourself, you're better equipped to take care of your family and meet your work responsibilities.

Finally, it's important to accept that balance doesn't mean perfection. There will be times when work overwhelms you, and times when a family needs to take center stage. What matters is not striving for an impossible ideal, but doing your best with the time and resources you have. Acknowledge the efforts you're making and be kind to yourself when things don't go as planned. Balancing work and family is an ongoing process, one that requires patience, flexibility, and a lot of love.

> *"If you want your children to be intelligent, read them fairy tales. If you want them to be more intelligent, read them more fairy tales."*

In the end, balancing work and family is about finding harmony in the midst of life's demands. It's about making intentional choices that reflect your values, setting boundaries that protect your time together, and staying connected through open communication and small gestures of love. By approaching this balance with care and mindfulness, you can create a life where both your career and your family thrive, where your relationships are strong, and where the people you love know they are always your top priority.

Guiding Through Emotional Turbulence: How to support your child through emotional ups and downs.

Parenting is a journey full of highs and lows, much like a ship navigating stormy seas. One of the most challenging aspects is guiding your child through their emotional ups and downs. Children experience a wide range of emotions, often with an intensity that can be overwhelming for both them and you. But with patience, empathy, and the right strategies, you can help them weather these storms and come out stronger on the other side.

The first step in supporting your child through emotional turbulence is to recognize that their feelings are real and valid, even if they seem small or irrational to you. What might seem like a minor issue in the grand scheme of things can feel like the end of the world to a child. Acknowledge their emotions without judgment. Instead of dismissing their feelings with phrases like "It's not a big deal" or "You'll get over it," try saying, "I can see that you're really upset about this." This simple acknowledgment goes a long way in making your child feel heard and understood.

Listening is crucial during these emotional moments. When your child is upset, resist the urge to jump in with advice or solutions. Sometimes, they just need someone to listen to their fears, frustrations, or sadness. Give them the space to express themselves fully. Maintain eye contact, nod, and offer comforting words like "I'm here for you" or "Tell me more about what's bothering you." By listening, you're not only validating their emotions but also helping them process their feelings.

However, it's not just about listening—it's about understanding. Try to get to the root of what's causing their distress. Ask open-ended questions that encourage them to explore their feelings more deeply. "What happened that made you feel this way?" or "How did that make you feel inside?" are good places to start. These questions help your child identify and articulate their emotions, which is a critical step in learning how to manage them.

Once your child has expressed their emotions, it's important to help them find ways to cope. This doesn't mean solving their problems for them, but rather equipping them with the tools they need to handle difficult emotions on their own. Teach them healthy coping mechanisms, such as taking deep breaths, counting to ten, or engaging in a physical activity like walking or stretching. These simple strategies can help them calm down and gain a sense of control over their emotions.

Sometimes, a child's emotional turbulence might be linked to something deeper, like anxiety or stress. In such cases, it's important to address the underlying issues rather than just the symptoms. For example, if your child is consistently anxious about school, talk to them about what specifically is causing that anxiety. Is it the fear of failure? Trouble with friends? Once you identify the root cause, you can work together to find solutions, whether it's offering extra support with homework, talking to a teacher, or helping them practice social skills.

Another key aspect of guiding your child through emotional ups and downs is modeling emotional resilience yourself. Children learn a lot by observing how you handle your own emotions. If you respond to stress with anger or frustration, they may learn to do the same. But if you approach challenges with calm and patience, they're likely to follow your lead. Be open about your own feelings and show them that it's okay to experience a range of emotions. Let them see how you cope with difficult situations, whether it's through taking a break, talking things out, or finding a positive outlet, like exercise or hobbies.

It's also important to set aside time for regular emotional check-ins. These don't have to be formal or structured—just moments where you ask your child how they're feeling and if there's anything on their mind. These check-ins create a safe space for your child to share their emotions before they become overwhelming. It also reinforces the idea that it's okay to talk about feelings and that they don't have to go through tough times alone.

Encourage your child to express their emotions through creative outlets. Drawing, writing, or playing music can be powerful ways for them to process and release their feelings. For some children, it's easier to express themselves through art than through words. Provide them with the tools and opportunities to explore these outlets. Not only does this help them manage their emotions, but it also fosters creativity and self-expression.

Teaching your child empathy is another way to help them navigate their own emotions. When they understand that others have feelings too, it can help them put their own emotions into perspective. Encourage them to consider how others might feel in similar situations. Ask questions like, "How do you think your friend felt when that happened?" This helps them develop a sense of empathy and compassion, which are essential skills for emotional intelligence.

However, there will be times when your child's emotions are overwhelming, and nothing seems to help. During these moments, just being there for them is enough. Hold them if they want to be held, sit with them in silence if they need quiet, and reassure them that it's okay to feel what they're feeling. Sometimes, the best support you can offer is simply your presence and unconditional love.

As your child grows, their emotional challenges will change. What seems like a big deal at age five might be forgotten by age ten, but new challenges will arise. Keep adapting your approach to meet their evolving needs. Stay patient, stay engaged, and continue to provide a stable, supportive environment where they feel safe expressing themselves.

Finally, remember that guiding your child through emotional turbulence is an ongoing process. There will be setbacks and difficult days, but each challenge is an opportunity for growth— for both you and your child. By consistently offering support, understanding, and love, you help them build the resilience they need to face life's ups and downs with confidence and grace. And in doing so, you strengthen the bond between you, creating a foundation of trust and security that will carry them through whatever storms may come.

"Although the world is full of suffering, it is also full of the overcoming of it."

CHAPTER TEN

CONCLUSION

Recap: The Emotional Journey of Parenting: Summarize the key takeaways and the importance of emotion in parenting.

Parenting is an emotional journey, one that takes you through a landscape of highs and lows, joys and challenges. It's a path filled with love, worry, pride, and sometimes frustration. As we reach the end of this exploration, it's time to reflect on the key lessons and the importance of emotions in the parenting process.

First and foremost, parenting is about connection. From the moment your child is born, the bond you share becomes the foundation for everything that follows. This connection is not just physical; it's emotional, rooted in love and trust. Building and maintaining this bond requires time, patience, and a deep understanding of your child's needs. It's about being present—not just physically, but emotionally—so your child feels safe, valued, and understood.

Throughout this book, we've explored the idea that emotions are the glue that holds families together. Whether it's through daily interactions, shared traditions, or the way you handle conflicts, the emotional environment you create at home shapes your child's development. Children learn how to express, manage, and understand their emotions by watching you. They mirror your reactions, absorb your moods, and internalize the values you model.

We've discussed the importance of emotional intelligence in parenting. Emotional intelligence isn't just a buzzword; it's a crucial skill that helps you understand your child's feelings, respond with empathy, and guide them through their emotional experiences. By cultivating emotional intelligence in yourself, you teach your child how to navigate their emotions effectively. This means being aware of your own feelings, recognizing when your child is struggling, and responding in a way that helps them feel supported.

Communication has been a recurring theme in our discussions. Open, honest, and respectful communication is the cornerstone of a healthy parent-child relationship. It's about listening as much as talking, about validating your child's feelings even when you don't fully understand them, and about setting boundaries that are clear yet compassionate. Good communication helps to build trust, resolve conflicts, and strengthen the emotional bond between you and your child.

Another key takeaway is the importance of consistency. Children thrive on routine and predictability, especially when it comes to emotional support. They need to know that no matter what happens, you'll be there for them. Consistency doesn't mean being perfect; it means being reliable. It's about showing up, day after day, in big ways and small. It's the daily rituals, the bedtime stories, the way you say goodnight, and the way you handle setbacks. These consistent acts of love and care create a stable emotional environment where your child feels secure.

We've also explored the challenges of balancing work and family life. In today's world, parents are often pulled in many directions, trying to juggle professional responsibilities with the demands of family. It's easy to feel overwhelmed or guilty when you can't be everything to everyone. But as we've seen, it's not about achieving a perfect balance—it's about finding a rhythm that works for your family. This means setting priorities, being present when you're with your family, and finding small ways to stay connected, even when life gets busy.

Guiding your child through emotional turbulence is another critical aspect of parenting. Children experience a wide range of emotions, from joy and excitement to fear and sadness. Helping them navigate these feelings is one of your most important roles as a parent. It's about teaching them that all emotions are valid, that it's okay to feel angry or scared, and that there are healthy ways to cope with these emotions. By being a steady presence in their lives, you give them the tools they need to manage their emotions and build resilience.

We've also touched on the role of cultural traditions in emotional development. In many families, traditions are the threads that connect generations, providing a sense of identity and belonging. Whether it's celebrating a festival, participating in religious rituals, or simply sharing stories from the past, these traditions reinforce the values and emotions that are important to your family. They teach your child about respect, gratitude, and the importance of community.

Finally, we've looked at the big picture—the idea that parenting is about raising not just happy children, but emotionally healthy adults. This means teaching your child how to handle life's ups and downs, how to build strong relationships, and how to live with integrity and compassion. It's about equipping them with the emotional tools they need to navigate the world, to face challenges with confidence, and to treat others with kindness.

As we conclude, it's important to remember that parenting is a journey without a fixed destination. There will be moments of triumph and moments of doubt, days when everything clicks and days when it feels like nothing is going right. But through it all, the love you share with your child will be the constant. It's the guiding star that will see you through the storms and lead you to calmer waters.

In the end, the emotional journey of parenting is not about getting everything right. It's about doing your best, learning from your mistakes, and showing your child that they are loved, no matter what. It's about creating a home where emotions are honored, where mistakes are forgiven, and where love is always the answer.

So, as you continue on this path, take these lessons to heart. Be kind to yourself and to your child. Celebrate the small victories and don't be afraid to ask for help when you need it. Remember that you are not alone on this journey—every parent faces challenges, and every parent has the strength to overcome them.

And most importantly, keep love at the center of everything you do. Because at the end of the day, it's love that matters most. It's the foundation upon which all else is built—the bedrock of trust, the source of joy, and the bond that will hold your family together through thick and thin.

> *"All, everything that I understand, I understand only because I love."*

As you move forward, let love guide your steps. With it, you'll find the strength to face any challenge, the wisdom to make the right choices, and the courage to lead your child with confidence and grace. This is the true essence of parenting, the emotional journey that will shape not just your child's life, but yours as well.

Embracing Emotional Parenting: Encouragement to continue fostering emotional bonds as your child grows.

Parenting is a lifelong journey, filled with moments that shape both you and your child. As your child grows, the way you connect with them evolves, but the foundation remains the same—emotional bonds. These bonds are the threads that weave your family together, creating a tapestry of shared experiences, trust, and love. Embracing emotional parenting isn't just a phase; it's a commitment that continues throughout your child's life.

As your child moves from one stage to the next, you might feel the pull to step back, to let them spread their wings. And that's natural. Independence is a crucial part of growing up. But as they venture out into the world, they still need to know that home is a place where their emotions are safe. Where they can return, no matter what, and be met with understanding and love.

Teenage years can be particularly challenging. Your once chatty child might become more withdrawn, more focused on friends than family. It's easy to feel like you're losing touch. But this is when your emotional bond matters most. Teenagers are navigating a minefield of new emotions, experiences, and pressures. They need to know that you're there, not just as a parent, but as someone who understands their struggles. Keep the lines of communication open. Even if it seems like they're pushing you away, be present. Show interest in their lives without being intrusive. Listen more than you talk. Sometimes, just knowing that you're available is enough.

As they transition into young adulthood, your role shifts again. Your child might be making decisions about college, careers, or relationships. These are big steps, often filled with uncertainty and fear. Your emotional support during this time can give them the confidence to take risks, to fail, and to try again. Be their sounding board, their safe haven. Offer guidance when asked, but more importantly, offer your belief in their ability to find their own way.

Even when your child reaches full adulthood, your emotional bond doesn't end—it deepens. The dynamic changes, but the need for connection remains. Adult children still seek their parents' approval, their advice, and their love. They might come to you with different kinds of problems—work stress, parenting challenges of their own, or relationship issues. Your experience, coupled with your ongoing emotional support, can be a guiding light. Remember, even grown-ups need their parents sometimes.

But emotional parenting isn't just about responding to your child's needs. It's about nurturing the relationship in ways that enrich both your lives. Continue to create moments of connection. Share meals, spend time together, and celebrate each other's successes. These moments, though they may seem ordinary, are the glue that keeps your bond strong. They remind your child that no matter how old they get, they're still your child, and you're still there for them.

It's also important to recognize that as your child grows, they'll develop their own emotional landscape. They might make choices you don't agree with, or they might express emotions in ways that are different from yours. This is where your emotional parenting skills are truly tested. It's easy to support a child who mirrors your values and beliefs; it's harder when they challenge them. But this is also where the depth of your bond can grow. Respect their individuality, even when it's difficult. Support their right to make their own choices, while still offering your wisdom and perspective.

In times of conflict, remember that your emotional connection is more important than being right. Disagreements are inevitable, but they don't have to weaken your bond. Approach these situations with empathy, with a focus on understanding rather than convincing. Your child will learn from how you handle these moments, and they'll carry those lessons into their own relationships.

As the years pass, you might find that the roles begin to reverse. There may come a time when your child becomes the one offering you emotional support. This is a natural part of the parenting journey, and it's a testament to the strength of the bond you've built. Accept their support with the same grace and love that you've shown them throughout their lives. Let them know that it's okay to take care of you, just as you've always taken care of them.

The journey of emotional parenting doesn't end—it simply changes shape. It's a dance that adjusts with time, with each phase of life bringing new challenges and new opportunities to connect. But through it all, the core remains the same: a commitment to love, to understanding, and to being there for each other, no matter what.

As you continue on this journey, remember that you don't have to be perfect. There will be times when you stumble, when you say the wrong thing, or when you don't know how to help. That's okay. What matters is that you keep trying, that you keep showing up, and that you keep loving your child with all your heart.

Emotional parenting is about more than just the big moments—it's about the everyday acts of love and support. It's about the bedtime stories, the hugs after a hard day, the late-night talks, and the quiet moments of just being together. These are the moments that build the foundation of your relationship, that create a bond strong enough to withstand the tests of time.

So, embrace this journey. Celebrate the highs, learn from the lows, and cherish the moments in between. Keep fostering those emotional bonds, because they are the ties that will hold your family together through all of life's changes. Your child might grow up, but they'll never outgrow the need for your love and support.

In the end, emotional parenting is about being there, in whatever way your child needs, as they navigate their own path through life. It's about offering a hand when they stumble, a shoulder when they cry, and a cheer when they succeed. It's about loving them unconditionally, through every phase, every challenge, and every triumph. And as you continue on this path, you'll find that the bond you've nurtured will not only strengthen your child but will also enrich your own life in ways you never imagined.

99

> *"At the end of the day, the most overwhelming key to a child's success is the positive involvement of parents."*

So, keep walking this journey with your child. Keep loving, keep supporting, and keep believing in the power of your bond.

Because in the end, that's what parenting is all about—being there, through thick and thin, with love that never wavers.

Looking Ahead: Your Child's Path Forward: Preparing for the next stages of your child's emotional and personal development.

As you look ahead, your child's path forward is filled with possibilities, challenges, and growth. Each stage of their life brings new opportunities for emotional and personal development. As a parent, your role is to prepare them for what lies ahead, to guide them as they step into the unknown, and to support them as they navigate the twists and turns of growing up.

The journey begins with understanding that your child's emotional development doesn't stop when they leave the early years behind. It evolves, becoming more complex as they encounter new experiences and responsibilities. From the playground to the classroom, from friendships to first jobs, each phase builds upon the last, shaping the person they will become.

One of the most critical stages in your child's path is adolescence. The teenage years are a whirlwind of emotions, identity exploration, and the quest for independence. It's a time when your child may seem to pull away, seeking more autonomy and relying less on your guidance. But beneath the surface, they still need your support more than ever. This is when they begin to form their own identity, testing boundaries and exploring who they are and who they want to be.

During this stage, it's essential to maintain open lines of communication. Encourage your teenager to express their thoughts and feelings, even if they're challenging or hard to hear. Listen without judgment, and offer advice when asked, but also allow them the space to make their own decisions. Mistakes will happen—let them. It's through these mistakes that they'll learn some of life's most important lessons. Your role is to provide a safety net, catching them when they fall and helping them get back up.

As your child transitions into young adulthood, their path forward involves making significant life choices—college, careers, relationships. These decisions can be overwhelming, and your guidance will be invaluable. However, it's important to shift from being the decision-maker to being a trusted advisor. Respect their choices, even if they differ from what you envisioned. Offer your wisdom, but also recognize that their path may lead in directions you didn't anticipate.

Encourage them to pursue their passions, to explore different paths, and to embrace the uncertainty that comes with adulthood. Remind them that it's okay to change course, to try something new, or to take risks. Life is not a straight line, and the detours often lead to the most rewarding destinations. Your support during this time can give them the confidence to follow their instincts and to trust in their own abilities.

Emotional resilience becomes increasingly important as your child steps into adulthood. They will face setbacks, disappointments, and challenges that will test their strength. Teach them that resilience isn't about never falling down—it's about getting back up each time they do. Share your own experiences with failure and how you overcame it. Help them see that setbacks are not the end, but rather opportunities to grow and learn.

As your child moves through these stages, their relationships will also play a significant role in their emotional development. Friendships, romantic relationships, and professional connections will all shape their sense of self and their understanding of the world. Encourage them to build strong, healthy relationships based on respect, trust, and mutual support. Teach them to value others' perspectives, to communicate openly, and to resolve conflicts with empathy and understanding.

At the same time, it's important to talk to them about the potential challenges of relationships—how to recognize toxic dynamics, set boundaries, and protect their own well-being. These conversations can be difficult, but they are crucial in helping your child navigate the complexities of human connections.

Looking ahead, another key aspect of your child's development is their sense of purpose. As they enter adulthood, they'll likely grapple with questions about what they want to do with their life, what they want to contribute to the world, and how they can find fulfillment. Support them in exploring these questions. Encourage them to reflect on their values, their passions, and their strengths. Whether they find purpose in their career, in their relationships, or in their hobbies, what matters most is that they feel a sense of meaning in what they do.

As they seek their path, remind them that success is not solely defined by external achievements—titles, salaries, or accolades. True success is finding peace within oneself, living in alignment with one's values, and building a life that feels authentic and fulfilling. Your guidance can help them see beyond the societal pressures and focus on what truly matters to them.

As a parent, one of your ongoing roles is to foster a lifelong love of learning in your child. Encourage them to stay curious, to seek knowledge, and to continue growing, no matter their age. Whether through formal education, travel, reading, or new experiences, the pursuit of learning keeps life vibrant and full of possibilities. Help them see that life is a continuous journey of discovery, where every experience is an opportunity to learn something new about themselves and the world around them.

Finally, as you prepare your child for the next stages of their emotional and personal development, remember that your relationship with them will continue to evolve. As they grow into adulthood, the dynamic between you will change, but the emotional bond you've built will remain a constant source of strength and support. Embrace this evolving relationship, celebrating the person they've become while also cherishing the deep connection that has always been there.

In conclusion, looking ahead at your child's path forward means recognizing that while the road may be uncertain, it's also filled with potential and growth. Your role as a parent is to be a steady presence, offering guidance, support, and love as they navigate their journey. Encourage them to take risks, to embrace challenges, and to trust in their own resilience. Remind them that they are never alone on this journey—you are there, cheering them on, ready to help when needed, but also confident in their ability to forge their own path.

The future is full of unknowns, but it's also full of opportunities. By preparing your child for the emotional and personal challenges that lie ahead, you're helping them build a foundation of confidence, resilience, and purpose. And as they step into this next chapter of their life, they carry with them the lessons, love, and support you've provided, ready to face whatever comes their way.

> *"The time is always right to do what is right."*

EPILOGUE

As we come to the end of this book, it's important to reflect on the journey we've shared. Parenting is not a destination; it's an ongoing process, filled with learning, growth, and endless opportunities to deepen the bonds you've built with your child. The lessons explored in these pages are meant to guide you, not just through the early years, but through the many stages of your child's life.

Throughout this book, we've emphasized the importance of emotional connection in parenting. We've discussed the ways in which love, empathy, and understanding form the foundation for your child's development. These emotional bonds are what will carry your child through life's challenges, giving them the confidence to explore, the strength to overcome obstacles, and the compassion to connect with others.

As you move forward, remember that parenting with the heart is about being present, not perfect. It's about showing up each day with love and patience, even when the path is difficult. It's about listening to your child, understanding their needs, and responding with kindness and support. And it's about forgiving yourself when things don't go as planned, knowing that every parent faces moments of doubt and uncertainty.

The emotional bonds you've nurtured will continue to grow as your child matures. There will be new challenges, new milestones, and new opportunities to connect. As your child steps into adolescence, young adulthood, and beyond, the foundation you've built will guide them. They'll carry the lessons of love and empathy with them, shaping the person they become and the relationships they build.

But parenting is not just about the child; it's also about you. This journey has likely changed you, too. It has tested your patience, expanded your capacity for love, and deepened your understanding of what it means to be a parent. It's a journey that will continue to shape you as your child grows, offering new insights and new ways to connect.

As you look ahead, take pride in the work you've done, the love you've given, and the bond you've created. Parenting is one of life's greatest challenges, but it is also one of its greatest rewards. The love you've invested in your child will not only help them thrive but will also create a legacy of compassion, understanding, and emotional strength that will be passed down through generations.

So, as you close this book, know that the journey of parenting with the heart doesn't end here. It continues every day, in the small moments of connection, in the challenges you face together, and in the love that binds you to your child. Keep nurturing that bond, keep showing up with love, and keep believing in the power of your connection.

Thank you for allowing me to be a part of your parenting journey. May your path be filled with love, joy, and the unbreakable bond of a parent's heart.

Surajit Sarkar
The 17th January, 2024

Acknowledgements

Writing "Parenting with Heart" has been a deeply fulfilling journey, one that would not have been possible without the support, encouragement, and inspiration of many wonderful people.

First and foremost, I want to express my heartfelt gratitude to the countless parents, children, and educators I've had the privilege of working with over the years. Your stories, challenges, and triumphs have provided the foundation for this book. Thank you for trusting me with your experiences and for teaching me as much as I have sought to teach you.

To my family, your unwavering love and support have been my anchor. To my parents, thank you for instilling in me the values of empathy, compassion, and the importance of family bonds. To my wife and children, your patience, understanding, and belief in me have been a constant source of strength. You are the heart of everything I do, and this book is as much yours as it is mine.

A special thanks to my colleagues and mentors who have guided me throughout my career. Your insights, feedback, and shared a passion for childhood development have shaped my approach to both teaching and writing. I am especially grateful to those who offered their time to review drafts and provide constructive feedback—your contributions have been invaluable.

To the Golden Childhood Institution, the school I founded and have devoted so much of my life to, thank you for being the living embodiment of the principles discussed in this book. The children and families we serve continue to inspire me every day. Your stories and experiences are woven throughout these pages, and I am deeply grateful for the role you've played in bringing this book to life.

I would also like to extend my gratitude to the editors and publishing team who believed in this project and worked tirelessly to bring it to fruition. Your expertise and dedication have helped shape this book into what it is today, and for that, I am truly thankful.

Lastly, to the readers of this book—thank you for taking the time to explore these ideas and for your commitment to parenting with heart. I hope this book provides you with the guidance, support, and inspiration you seek as you navigate the incredible journey of raising emotionally healthy children.

With deep appreciation,

Surajit Sarkar
The 17th January, 2024

About the Author

Surajit Sarkar is a distinguished educator, counselor, and advocate for childhood development with over three decades of experience in the field. Born and raised in West Bengal, India, Surajit has dedicated his life to understanding the emotional and psychological needs of children and guiding parents in nurturing these essential aspects of development.

In 1996, Surajit founded the Golden Childhood Institution in Maynaguri, West Bengal, a school dedicated to fostering the holistic growth of children. The institution has since become a beacon of innovative educational practices and emotional support, positively impacting countless children and their families.

Surajit holds a strong academic background in science, complemented by deep expertise in positive psychology, medical hypnosis, and Neuro-Linguistic Programming (NLP). His unique blend of scientific knowledge and practical experience has made him a sought-after expert in the field of emotional and psychological development. He is also a Fellow in Cardiac Rehabilitation from Apollo Hospital, Hyderabad, reflecting his commitment to holistic well-being.

A prolific writer, Surajit has authored several books on childhood development and parenting, including the well-received "Nurturing Bonds: A Handbook for Emotional Development in Early Childhood" and "Emotional Edge in Parenting: Your Complete Guide to Childhood Education". His writing is known for its empathy, practical wisdom, and deep understanding of the challenges and joys of parenting.

Surajit is an active member of various career counseling and psychological organizations, both in India and internationally. His work has been instrumental in shaping modern approaches to parenting and education, particularly in the context of emotional intelligence and mental well-being. He had been a member of 'British Society of Experimental and Clinical Hypnosis' and the 'International Hypnosis Federation'.

When he's not writing or working with children and parents, Surajit enjoys spending time with his family, engaging in community service, and exploring the natural beauty of West Bengal. His lifelong passion for education, combined with his personal and professional experiences, continues to inspire his work and his commitment to helping families build strong, loving relationships.

Through "Parenting with Heart: Emotional Bonds for Early Childhood Development", Surajit Sarkar shares his insights and strategies for raising emotionally healthy children, offering parents the tools and understanding they need to create lasting, meaningful connections with their children.

BIBLIOGRAPHY

Books and Articles on Emotional Bonding and Attachment:

1. **Bowlby, John.** *Attachment and Loss: Vol. 1, Attachment.* Basic Books, 1969. *[A foundational work in the study of attachment theory, detailing the importance of early bonds between parents and children.]*

2. **Ainsworth, Mary D.S., et al.** *Patterns of Attachment: A Psychological Study of the Strange Situation.* Lawrence Erlbaum Associates, 1978. *[This book presents research on different types of attachment and their long-term effects on children's emotional development.]*

Books on Early Childhood Development:

3. **Piaget, Jean.** *The Origins of Intelligence in Children.* International Universities Press, 1952. *[Piaget's work on cognitive development provides a framework for understanding how children learn and grow intellectually and emotionally.]*

4. **Erikson, Erik H.** *Childhood and Society.* W.W. Norton & Company, 1950. *[Erikson's stages of psychosocial development highlight the importance of early emotional bonds in personality development.]*

Parenting Techniques and Strategies:

5. **Sears, William, and Martha Sears.** *The Attachment Parenting Book: A Commonsense Guide to Understanding and Nurturing Your Baby.* Little, Brown and Company, 2001. *[A practical guide that outlines attachment parenting practices and their benefits for child development.]*

6. **Montessori, Maria.** *The Absorbent Mind.* Holt, Rinehart and Winston, 1967. *[Montessori's insights into early childhood education stress the importance of a nurturing environment for emotional and intellectual growth.]*

Cultural Influences on Parenting:

7. **Rogoff, Barbara.** *The Cultural Nature of Human Development.* Oxford University Press, 2003. *[This book explores how culture shapes the way children develop and learn, emphasizing the role of social context in parenting.]*

8. **Cole, Michael, and Sheila R. Cole.** *The Development of Children.* Worth Publishers, 1993. *[Offers a comprehensive overview of child development with an emphasis on the influence of cultural practices.]*

Psychology and Emotional Intelligence:

9. **Goleman, Daniel.** *Emotional Intelligence: Why It Can Matter More Than IQ.* Bantam Books, 1995. *[Goleman's exploration of emotional intelligence underscores its significance in parenting and child development.]*

10. **Siegel, Daniel J., and Tina Payne Bryson.** *The Whole-Brain Child: 12 Revolutionary Strategies to Nurture Your Child's Developing Mind.* Delacorte Press, 2011. *[This book integrates neuroscience with parenting strategies to foster emotional and cognitive development in children.]*

Research on Play and Physical Activity:

11. **Elkind, David.** *The Power of Play: Learning What Comes Naturally.* Da Capo Lifelong Books, 2007. *[Elkind discusses the critical role of play in emotional and cognitive development.]*

12. **Pellegrini, Anthony D., and Peter K. Smith.** *The Nature of Play: Great Apes and Humans.* Guilford Press, 2005. *[A comprehensive examination of the role of play in development from an evolutionary and psychological perspective.]*

Mindfulness and Parenting:

13. **Kabat-Zinn, Jon.** *Mindful Parenting: Understanding the Importance of Being Present in Your Child's Life.* Hachette Books, 1997. *[Discusses the benefits of mindfulness practices for parents in fostering a strong, emotionally connected family environment.]*

General Parenting and Family Dynamics:

14. **Baumrind, Diana.** *Parenting Styles and Their Effects on Children.* Journal of Clinical Child Psychology, 1991. *[Provides an*

analysis of different parenting styles and their impact on child development and behaviour.]

15. **Satir, Virginia.** *The New Peoplemaking.* Science and Behaviour Books, 1988. *[Focuses on family dynamics and the importance of communication and emotional bonds within the family structure.]*

www.ingramcontent.com/pod-product-compliance
Lightning Source LLC
Chambersburg PA
CBHW041327120726
48005CB00014B/2149